Contents

Preface

The purpose of this text is to provide a repository of information about fractions and their associated surroundings. Parentheses are used to indicate multiplication as well as a convenient method of grouping numbers together. Underlining is used to draw attention to specific text or numeric information.

Background - During 16 years of volunteer math tutoring, mostly high school students, as well as GED, HISET, and grammar school students, I found that the lack of arithmetic comprehension seems to be almost universal. I also discovered the lack of comprehension of the subject of mathematics exists across the entire student age range background spectrum. Arithmetic and mathematics teaching and education is provided and/or taught with an emphasis on just how much this subject should be disliked and avoided. The idea that math is a loathed subject, is fostered as such, resulting in a void of comprehension and an extensive lack of retention. Additionally, many of the instructors and teachers observed during these years have a limited comprehension of this subject matter as well.

The most common difficulty for students I have experienced are adding and subtracting signed numbers, followed by multiplication, fractions and fractions to decimal conversion, long division, decimal to fraction conversion, and percentages. Exponents, square roots and logarithms are almost completely unknown to most students. There are exceptions of course; however, in my experience, I estimate these exceptions could be outnumbered by as much as 20 to 40 to 1, perhaps more.

The learning environment, home, school, friends, nearly everywhere, permeates with the idea that math is difficult along with the expressions of "I dislike, loath, or despise math". No wonder many if not most students fare poorly, while few students excel in the subject. The student is taught in a subliminal manner and becomes predisposed to the idea that arithmetic and mathematics, in general, is a difficult subject. And so it becomes self-fulfilling.

Dictionary

- **Common Denominator**
  - The same denominator value for all fractions involved in the operation
  - Common denominators are required for addition and subtraction of fractions

- **Composite Number**
  - A positive integer whole number which is the product of at least 2 integer whole number
  - see list of first 75 composite numbers in appendix

- **Cube Root**
  - The cube root of a number is that value which when multiplied by itself 3 times produces the original number
  - example, $\sqrt[3]{8} = 2$, **then** $2 \times 2 \times 2 = 8$

- **Denominator**
  - The bottom number or the number below the dividing line of the fraction

- **Dividing Line**
  - The line which separates the numerator from the denominator in a fraction

- **Even Numbers**
  - Numbers when divided by 2 leave no fractional remainder or leave a remainder of 0
  - Numbers 0, 2, 4, 6, or 8 are even numbers

- **Exponents**
  - A number indicating repeated multiplication that is how many times a number is multiplied by itself

- **Expression**
  - A combination of numbers including at least 1 operation, example, $3 \times (7+9)$

- **GCD**
  - Greatest Common Denominator

- **Improper Fraction**
  - A fraction where the numerator is greater than (larger than) the denominator

- **Integer**
  - A number without fractional parts
  - Any positive or negative whole number
  - examples, 1, 7, 43, 456, −6, −56, −7,351, 0
    - Note, 0 is an integer, however, it is neither positive or negative
    - Note, fractions, and decimal numbers are NOT integers

- **Inversion**   • **Invert**
  - Same as invert (see reciprocal below)

- **LCD**
  - Least or Lowest Common Denominator

- **LCM**
  - Least or Lowest Common Multiple

- **Mixed Number**
  - An <u>integer whole number</u> followed by a <u>fraction</u> located to the right of the whole number

- **Multiplier**
  - When two numbers are multiplied together one number is the <u>Multiplier</u> the other number is the <u>Multiplicand</u>

- **Multiplicand**
  - See Multiplier above

- **Numerator**
  - The top number or the number above the dividing line of a fraction

- **Odd Numbers**
  - Odd numbers end in 1, 3, 5, 7, or 9
  - A number which cannot be evenly divided by the number 2
  - Note, evenly divided by 2 means divided by 2 with a remainder of 0

- **Operations**
  - Addition, Subtraction, Multiplication, Division, Exponentiation, Squaring, Square Root, Inversion, Reciprocation, Differentiation, and Integration are common mathematical operations.

- **Order of Operations**
  - When 2 or more arithmetic operations are necessary, the order of operations (the sequence of which operation comes first, and which operations follow which operations, and direction, left to right, right to left, and top to bottom) is important
  - To help remember the order, the first letter of each operation, listed in order of operation, is used as a reminder
  - Parentheses **(P)**, are always first, followed by Exponents **(E)**, including squares and square roots, followed by Multiplication **(M)**, and Division **(D)**, then Addition **(A)**, and Subtraction **(S)**
    • **PEMDAS**
  - Notes • parentheses are evaluated innermost parentheses first • Exponents are evaluated top to bottom • Multiplication and division evaluated left to right • Addition and subtraction evaluated left to right

- **Parentheses**
  - Parentheses ( ) allow items and operations to be grouped together. • Parentheses are typically used to indicate multiplication. • Square brackets **[ ]** and curly brackets **{ }** can be used as well • see order of operations above

- **PEMDAS**
  - see order of operations above

- **Prime Number**
  - A number which can only be divided evenly by itself or 1 • examples, 2, 3, 5, 7, 11, 13, 17, 19, 23, 29, 31, 37, 41
  - Note, except for 2 and 5, all prime numbers end in 1, 3, 7, or 9
  - Note, see list of first 1000 prime numbers in appendix

- **Proper Fractions**
  - A fraction where the numerator is less than (smaller than) the denominator

- **Reciprocal**
  - Exchange or swap numerator and denominator • Related values such that their product is 1, example

$$\left(\frac{2}{3} \times \frac{3}{2} \right) = 1$$

- **Square Root**
  - The square root of a number is that value which when multiplied by itself produces the original number
  - example, $\sqrt[2]{9} = 3$, then $3 * 3 = 9$

- **Whole Number**
  - Any positive integer, also known as counting number, and natural numbers
  - examples include, 1, 2, 3, 101, 2,012, 9,876, 543, 0
  - Note, 0 is an integer, however, it is neither positive or negative
  - Note, fractions, decimals, and negative numbers are not whole numbers

Arithmetic Notations, Key Words, Operations, Symbols, etc.

- **Words that mean *ADDITION***
  - Add, Sum, Plus, Total, Combine, All Together
  - More than, Increase by

- **Words that mean *SUBTRACTION***
  - Minus, Difference, Decrease, Less, From, Less than
  - Decrease by, Reduce by, Subtract from
  - How much more than

- **Words and Notation that mean *MULTIPLICATION***
  - Times, Product, Multiply by, Twice as much
  - Multiples of a number, examples, 5 times as much
  - 8 times as much, 11 times as much
  - notation for multiplication, example, **(A times B)**
  - **AB   A*B   (A)*(B)   (A)(B)   A(B)**

- **What is *MULTIPLICATION?***
  - Multiplication is a process that simplifies repeated addition
  - example add 2 to itself 5 times, $2 + 2 + 2 + 2 + 2 = 10$
  - multiplying 5 times 2 provide identical results, $(5 \times 2) = 10$

- **Words that mean *DIVISION***
  - Divide by, Quotient, Factor, Factors of Ratio of
  - example, a ratio of 2 to 1

- **Words that mean *EXPONENTIATION***
  - Squared,   Cubed,   4th Power,   Power of
  - Raised to the power of, Up

- **Symbol that mean *APPROXIMATELY***
  - $\approx$

- **Symbol in this text that mean more digits . . .**
  - Example, **three spaced periods** following the last digit to the right of the decimal point indicates more digits to follow
  - Example, $\sqrt[2]{2} = \mathbf{1.4142135 \ . \ . \ .}$

- **Companion Document**
  - *ALL ABOUT FRACTIONS* AND MORE *Solution to Problems*
  - Solutions and answers to all problems are located in this document

- **Appendix**
  - Appendix A – J

Parentheses, Signed Whole Numbers, Signed Fractions

- Examples of signed whole numbers, **+31, −22, −762, −(3 − 29)**
- Note, an integer, or whole number, without a sign is always a positive number

---

- Examples of signed fractions $\quad \dfrac{-2}{3}, \quad -\left(\dfrac{-7}{16}\right), \quad +\left(\dfrac{-3}{8}\right), \quad \left(\dfrac{-5+19}{23}\right)$

- Fractions or fractional expressions without a sign are always positive fractions
- Order of operations requires innermost parentheses and brackets first
- Reference **PEMDAS** in the dictionary above.
- If the sign in front of the parentheses is <u>Positive</u> don't change the signs inside the parentheses, just execute the operations and eliminate the parentheses
- If the sign in front of the parentheses is <u>Negative</u>, (1st), reverse all the signs inside that parentheses, (2nd), change the sign in front of that parentheses to positive, and (3rd), execute the operations and eliminate the parentheses

---

- Sign, parentheses, and simplification examples
- $\quad -(-) = + \qquad -(+) = - \qquad\qquad +(-) = - \qquad\qquad +(+) = +$

- **EXAMPLES,**

$-(3-29) = +(-3+29) = +26 \qquad +(-14+9) = +(-5) = -5$

$-\left(\dfrac{-7}{16}\right) = \left(\dfrac{+7}{16}\right) = \dfrac{+7}{16} \ OR + \dfrac{7}{16} \ OR \ \dfrac{7}{16} \qquad\qquad +\left(\dfrac{-3}{8}\right) = \dfrac{-3}{8} \ OR - \left(\dfrac{3}{8}\right)$

$-\left(+31 - (-27+17)\right) = -\left(+31+(+27-17)\right) = -(+31+10) = -(+41) =$

$= -(+41) = +(-41) = -41$

$-\dfrac{7}{8}\left(-4\dfrac{3}{7}\right) / \left(+2\dfrac{4}{10}\right) = -\dfrac{7}{8}\left(-\dfrac{31}{7}\right) / \left(+\dfrac{24}{10}\right) = -\left(\dfrac{7}{8}\right) \times -\left(\dfrac{31}{7}\right) \times \left(\dfrac{10}{24}\right) =$

$= +\left(\dfrac{(7\times31\times10)}{(8\times7\times24)}\right) = \dfrac{310}{192} = \dfrac{310/2}{192/2} = \dfrac{155}{96} = 1\dfrac{55}{96}$

$4\dfrac{1}{8}$ means add, the same as $4 + \dfrac{1}{8} = \left(\dfrac{(4 \times 8)}{(1 \times 8)} + \dfrac{1}{8}\right) = \left(\dfrac{(32 + 1)}{8}\right) = \dfrac{33}{8} = 4\dfrac{1}{8}$

$4 - \dfrac{1}{8}$ means subtract $= \left(\dfrac{(4 \times 8)}{(1 \times 8)} - \dfrac{1}{8}\right) = \left(\dfrac{(32 - 1)}{8}\right) = \dfrac{31}{8} = 3\dfrac{7}{8}$

$4\left(\dfrac{-1}{8}\right)$ means multiply $= \left(\dfrac{4}{1}\right) \times \left(\dfrac{-1}{8}\right) = \left(\dfrac{4}{1}\right) \times -\left(\dfrac{1}{8}\right) = -\left(\dfrac{(4 \times 1)}{(1 \times 8)}\right) = -\dfrac{4}{8} = -\dfrac{1}{2}$

Adding and Subtracting Signed Whole Numbers

- When signs are the <u>same</u>
- Keep the sign of either number
- <u>Add</u> the numbers together

- **EXAMPLES**

$3 + 4 = 7$

$-5 - 8 = -13$

$+4 + 5 = +9$

$-31 - (+18) = -49$

$-7 - 2 = -9$

- When signs are <u>different</u>   • Keep the sign of the <u>larger</u> number
- <u>Subtract</u> the smaller number from the larger number

- **EXAMPLES**

$8 - 5 = 3$

$5 - 8 = -3$

$-16 - (+3) = -19$

$+11 - 7 = +4$

$-16 + 3 = -13$

$-12 - (-15) = +3$

$-7 + 2 = -5$

$-12 + 15 = +3$

- Note, a number without a sign is always a positive number

- **Parentheses,** $-(-) = +$ $-(+) = -$ $+(-) = -$ $+(+) = +$

- **PRACTICE**

$9 + 18 = \underline{\hspace{2cm}}$

$-8 - 9 = \underline{\hspace{2cm}}$

$-3 - 11 = \underline{\hspace{2cm}}$

$+11 - 12 = \underline{\hspace{2cm}}$

$-(-7) + (-29) = \underline{\hspace{1.5cm}}$

$4 - (+7) = \underline{\hspace{2cm}}$

$+7 - 16 = \underline{\hspace{2cm}}$

$21 - 19 = \underline{\hspace{2cm}}$

$-3 + 14 = \underline{\hspace{2cm}}$

$-3 + (-14) = \underline{\hspace{1.5cm}}$

$(-9 + 27) = \underline{\hspace{1.5cm}}$

$-3 + 14 = \underline{\hspace{2cm}}$

$-18 + 5 = \underline{\hspace{2cm}}$

$-4 - (-9) = \underline{\hspace{1.5cm}}$

$+4 + 5 = \underline{\hspace{2cm}}$

$-(-3) + (-19) = \underline{\hspace{1.5cm}}$

Multiplying and Dividing Signed Whole Numbers

- When multiplying or dividing numbers with the <u>same signs</u> the result is always <u>POSITIVE</u>

- **EXAMPLES**

$4 \times 3 = 12$

$14 / 7 = 2$

$24 / +6 = +4$

$-3 \times -5 = +15$

$+9 / 3 = +3$

$+8 \times +4 = +32$

$-26 / -2 = 13$

- When multiplying or dividing numbers with the <u>different signs</u> the result is always <u>NEGATIVE</u>

- **EXAMPLES**

$(4 \times -3) = -12$

$(14 / -7) = -2$

$-24 / -(-6) = -4$

$(-3 \times 5) = -15$

$-(+9) / 3) = -3$

$-(+87) / +(-3) = +29$

$8 \times +(-4) = -32$

$-26 / 2 = -13$

- Note, a number without a sign is always a positive number

- **Parentheses,** $-\left(-\right) = +$ $\qquad -\left(+\right) = -$ $\qquad +\left(-\right) = -$ $\qquad +\left(+\right) = +$

- **PRACTICE**

$17 \times 3 =$ _____

$9 \times 4 =$ _____

$+54 / -9 =$ _____

$+129 / -43 =$ _____

$+(-46) \div -(+23) =$ _____

$-19 \times 7 / 76 =$ _____

$-(-12) / -3 =$ _____

$-39 / -3 =$ _____

$78 / -13 =$ _____

$-91 / +13 =$ _____

$78 / -(13 \times -3) =$ _____

$5\left(-23\right) \div -\left(-46\right) =$ _____

$-27 / 9 =$ _____

$-42 / (-(-6)) =$ _____

$-13 (-7 + 23) / 19 =$ _____

$-84 / -6 =$ _____

$(45 + 9) / (-9) =$ _____

$78 / -(13 \times -3) =$ _____

What Is a Fraction?

- A fraction indicates a part of something or parts of the total
- A fraction has two (2) numbers
- The number above the <u>dividing line</u> is the NUMERATOR
  - The numerator indicated how many parts of the total
- The number below the <u>dividing line</u> is the DENOMINATOR
  - The denominator indicated total number of parts

- **EXAMPLES**

$\dfrac{2}{3}$ **means 2 parts of a total of 3 parts**

$\dfrac{7}{16}$ **means 7 parts of a total of 16 parts**

$\dfrac{5}{4}$ **means 5 parts of a total of 4 parts** $= \dfrac{5}{4} = 1\dfrac{1}{4}$

- Note, 5/4 is an improper fraction because the numerator is greater than the denominator.

- Note, 4/4 is an improper fraction because the numerator is equal to the denominator, and the value is equal to 1

- Note, see Dictionary for definition of Proper and Improper fractions

---

Proper and Improper Fraction

- **Proper Fraction**, the numerator is less, or smaller than the denominator
- The value of a proper fraction is less than 1.
- **Improper Fraction**, the numerator is greater than (or larger than) or equal to the denominator
- The value of an improper fraction is greater than or equal to 1.
- Improper fractions can be changed to mixed numbers by dividing the larger numerator by the smaller denominator.
- If there is a remainder from the result of the division, it is the numerator of the fraction part of the mixed number.

- **EXAMPLES**

$$\frac{11}{8} = 1\frac{3}{8} \qquad\qquad \frac{15}{7} = 2\frac{1}{7} \qquad\qquad \frac{23}{16} = 1\frac{7}{16}$$

- **EXAMPLE**

$$\frac{28}{9} = \frac{(27+1)}{9} = \left(\frac{27}{9} + \frac{1}{9}\right) = \left(3 + \frac{1}{9}\right) = 3\frac{1}{9}$$

- **PRACTICE**
- change the improper fractions to mixed numbers

$$\frac{23}{7} = \qquad\qquad \frac{7}{4} = \qquad\qquad \frac{19}{5} = \qquad\qquad \frac{29}{11} =$$

$$\frac{28}{17} = \qquad\qquad \frac{11}{4} = \qquad\qquad \frac{33}{8} = \qquad\qquad \frac{18}{16} =$$

$$\frac{37}{19} = \qquad\qquad \frac{29}{9} = \qquad\qquad \frac{43}{6} = \qquad\qquad \frac{23}{12} =$$

Mixed Numbers
(Whole Number plus Fraction)

- A mixed number is an integer (whole number) followed by a fraction located to the right of the integer whole number

---

- **EXAMPLES**

$$4\frac{1}{3} \text{ same as } 4 + \frac{1}{3} \qquad\qquad -5\frac{7}{16} \text{ same as } -\left(5 + \frac{7}{16}\right)$$

- A mixed number can be changed to an improper fraction by adding the numerator to the product of the whole number times the denominator.
- The result is placed over the denominator

- **EXAMPLES**

$$2\frac{3}{8} = \frac{(2 \times 8) + 3}{8} = \frac{19}{8} \qquad\qquad 7\frac{4}{9} = \frac{(7 \times 9) + 4}{9} = \frac{67}{9}$$

$$5\frac{3}{4} = \left(\frac{5 \times 4}{4} + \frac{3}{4}\right) = \frac{20 + 3}{4} = \frac{23}{4}$$

- **PRACTICE**
- change mixed numbers to improper fractions,

$2\frac{4}{5} = \underline{\hspace{1cm}}$ $\qquad$ $3\frac{7}{8} = \underline{\hspace{1cm}}$ $\qquad$ $9\frac{2}{3} = \underline{\hspace{1cm}}$ $\qquad$ $11\frac{9}{11} = \underline{\hspace{1cm}}$

$22\frac{1}{3} = \underline{\hspace{1cm}}$ $\qquad$ $31\frac{1}{4} = \underline{\hspace{1cm}}$ $\qquad$ $5\frac{6}{7} = \underline{\hspace{1cm}}$ $\qquad$ $11\frac{3}{4} = \underline{\hspace{1cm}}$

$9\frac{7}{16} = \underline{\hspace{1cm}}$ $\qquad$ $6\frac{6}{5} = \underline{\hspace{1cm}}$ $\qquad$ $8\frac{13}{7} = \underline{\hspace{1cm}}$ $\qquad$ $17\frac{11}{3} = \underline{\hspace{1cm}}$

$13\frac{3}{8} = \underline{\hspace{1cm}}$ $\qquad$ $9\frac{1}{6} = \underline{\hspace{1cm}}$ $\qquad$ $7\frac{2}{9} = \underline{\hspace{1cm}}$

Adding and Subtracting Fractions with the Same Denominator

- Fractions can only be added or subtracted together if the denominators are the same.
- If the denominators are the same, the values of the numerators can be added or subtracted together and placed above either denominator
  - **Note, see next for different denominators**

- **EXAMPLES**

- $\dfrac{1}{6} + \dfrac{4}{6} = \dfrac{1+4}{6} = \dfrac{5}{6}$

- $\dfrac{5}{9} + \dfrac{-3}{9} = \dfrac{5-3}{9} = \dfrac{2}{9}$

- $\dfrac{4}{5} - \dfrac{1}{5} = \dfrac{4-1}{5} = \dfrac{3}{5}$

- $\dfrac{-2}{11} - \dfrac{-7}{11} = \dfrac{-2+7}{11} = \dfrac{+5}{11} = \dfrac{5}{11}$

- **PRACTICE**

- $\dfrac{11}{7} - \dfrac{5}{7} =$ _____

- $\dfrac{4}{21} + \dfrac{13}{21} =$ _____

- $\dfrac{-3}{8} - \dfrac{5}{8} =$ _____

- $\dfrac{4}{13} - \dfrac{+3}{13} =$ _____

- $\dfrac{13}{17} + \dfrac{3}{17} =$ _____

- $\dfrac{7}{19} - \dfrac{13}{19} =$ _____

- $\dfrac{13}{15} + \dfrac{-4}{15} =$ _____

- $\dfrac{-9}{14} - \dfrac{-3}{14} =$ _____

Adding and Subtracting Fractions with Different Denominator

- Since fractions can **ONLY** be added or subtracted together if all the denominators are the **SAME**, one or more of all the fractions must be changed to make all the denominators of all the fractions the same
- This can be accomplished by finding a Common Denominator for all the fractions without changing the value of the fraction
- One method of finding a common denominator is to simply multiply all the denominators together
- This will always produce a common denominator, however, it may not be the smallest, lowest, or least common denominator

---

- **EXAMPLE**

(1/3) + (2/5) cannot be added together until the denominators are the same • Multiplying the denominators 3 and 5 together provides a common denominator of 15. • This is accomplished by multiplying both numerator and denominator of each fraction by the denominator of the opposite fraction allowing the value of the fraction to remain unchanged

- $\dfrac{1}{3} + \dfrac{2}{5} = \left(\dfrac{1}{3} \times \dfrac{5}{5}\right) + \left(\dfrac{2}{5} \times \dfrac{3}{3}\right) = \dfrac{5}{15} + \dfrac{6}{15} = \dfrac{11}{15}$

- **EXAMPLE**

(3/4) + (5/12) cannot be added together until the denominators are the same. • Multiplying the denominators 4 and 12 together provides a common denominator of 48, and it is a common denominator and it will work, however, it is not the lowest common denominator. • Since the denominator 4 is a factor of the denominator 12, 12 can be a common denominator for both fractions, and is the lowest common denominator for these two fractions

- $\dfrac{3}{4} + \dfrac{5}{12} = \left(\dfrac{3}{4} \times \dfrac{3}{3}\right) + \dfrac{5}{12} = \dfrac{9}{12} + \dfrac{5}{12} = \dfrac{14}{12} = 1\dfrac{2}{12} = 1\dfrac{1}{6}$

- **PRACTICE**

- $\dfrac{5}{6} - \dfrac{3}{4} =$ _____

- $\dfrac{5}{8} + \dfrac{7}{12} =$ _____

- $\dfrac{11}{18} - \left(\dfrac{-5}{6}\right) =$ _____

- $\dfrac{-13}{17} + \dfrac{-6}{34} =$ _____

- $-\dfrac{11}{12} + \left(\dfrac{-3}{4}\right) =$ _____

- $\dfrac{-18}{9} - \dfrac{-10}{27} =$ _____

- $\dfrac{13}{21} + \dfrac{5}{7} =$ _____

- $\dfrac{11}{6} - \dfrac{3}{4} =$ _____

Finding a Common Denominator and Finding the Lowest Common Denominator (LCD)

- What is a Common Denominator?
- What is the Least or Lowest Common Denominator, the LCD?
- When the denominator (bottom number of a fraction) of 2 or more fractions are the same, they are said to have common denominators

---

- **EXAMPLE**

Fractions **2/3**, **3/4**, and **5/6** do not have common denominators, however, they can be changed to have common denominators by selecting 12, 24, 36, or 72, as a new denominator because any of these 4 numbers can be **<u>evenly divided</u>** by denominators 3, 4, and 6, of the 3 fractions, without leaving a remainder

12/3 = 4	24/3 = 8	36/3 = 12	72/3 = 24
12/4 = 3	24/4 = 6	36/4 = 9	72/4 = 18
12/6 = 2	24/6 = 4	36/6 = 6	72/6 = 12

- Although any of these 4 common denominators, 12, 24, 36, or 72, can be used, the lowest value common denominator, **12**, is the most optimum and best choice, and is the **(LCD)**
- **(2/3) × (4/4) = 8/12,   (3/4) × (3/3) = 9/12, and (5/6) × (2/2) = (10/12)**
- Although the numbers of the fractions have changes the original value of each fraction remains unchanged
- Since the three fractions now have common denominators they can be added or subtracted together as required.
- Other names for Lowest Common Denominator include Smallest, Least, or Lower Common Denominator

---

- The Lease or Lowest Common Denominator (LCD) is the <u>smallest or lowest integer number</u> that can be divided by the denominators of 2 or more fractions evenly without leaving a remainder, or by leaving a remainder of 0

Finding the Least Common Multiple (LCM)

- LCM is the general term applying to the lowest or least common multiple of any group of integer numbers
- The Least Common Multiple (**LCM**) is the smallest positive integer that is evenly divisible by two or more quantities
- The LCM is the same as the LCD when considering fractions and the denominator of the fraction
- Although Least Common Denominator (**LCD**) is typically used when discussing fractions, LCM would not be incorrect or inaccurate
- Other names include Smallest, Lower, or Lowest Common Multiple

---

- **EXAMPLE**

The LCM of numbers (3, 4, 7, and 10) is **420** since it is the smallest, lowest, and least value of any, and all possible, common multiples that all 4 numbers can evenly divided
- note, evenly divided means leaving no remainder or a remainder of 0
- $420/3 = 140$, $420/4 = 105$, $420/7 = 60$, $420/10 = 42$
- Other common multiples include multiples of 420, that is, 840, 1260, etc.
- $840/3 = 280$, $840/4 = 210$, $840/7 = 120$, $840/10 = 84$
- $1260/3 = 420$, $1260/4 = 315$, $1260/7 = 180$, $1260/10 = 126$

- One method of finding a common multiple of 2 or more numbers or 2 or more denominators is to multiply all the quantities together
- In the example above, (numbers 3, 4, 7, 10) the combined product of the 4 numbers is **840** and although it is a common multiple it is not the LCM
- The direct and optimum method for finding the LCM of two or more quantities is to multiply together <u>only</u> the <u>highest power of prime numbers</u> present in each number
- In the example above, (numbers 3, 4, 7, 10) the primes are, (3^1), (2^2), (7^1), (2^1), and (5^1), the product is $3^1 \times 2^2 \times 7^1 \times 5^1 = 420$
- Since (2^2) is the highest power of the prime 2, and the prime (2^1) is contained in the (2^2) prime, the <u>(2^1) is not the highest power</u> of that prime, and <u>is not used</u> in the multiplication

---

Greatest Common Factor (GCF) and Greatest Common Divisor (GCD)

- The Greatest Common Divisor **(GCD)** of two or more nonzero integers is the largest positive nonzero integer that divides each of the integers evenly
- note, evenly divided means leaving no remainder or a remainder of 0
- GCD or GCF is typically presented as gcd(a,b,c)
- Other names include • Greatest Common Factor (GCF)
- Greatest Common Measure (GCM) • Highest Common Factor (HCF)

- GCD is the same as GCF when discussing fractions and the denominators of the fractions
  - Although GCD is typically used when discussing fractions, GCF would not be incorrect nor inaccurate
- Greatest Common Factor (GCF) is a more general name
- Other names include • Greatest Common Measure (GCM) • Highest Common Factor (HCF)

- **EXAMPLES**
- gcf(8, 14, 32) = 2 since 2 is the common factor of all 3 numbers
  - prime factors of 8 are **2, 2, and 2** ($2 \times 2 \times 2 = 8$)
  - prime factors of 14 are **2 and 7** ($2 \times 7 = 14$)
  - prime factors of 32 are **2, 2, 2, 2, and 2** ($2 \times 2 \times 2 \times 2 \times 2 = 32$)

- gcf(9, 12, 33) = 3 since 3 is the common factor of all 3 numbers
  - prime factors of 9 are **3 and 3** ($3 \times 3 = 9$)
  - prime factors of 12 are **2, 2, and 3** ($2 \times 2 \times 3 = 12$)
  - prime factors of 33 are **3 and 11** ($3 \times 11 = 33$)

- gcf(22, 121, 198, 264) = 11 since 11 is the common factor of all 4 numbers
  - prime factors of 22 are **2 and 11**, ($2 \times 11 = 22$)
  - prime factors of 121 are **11, 11** ($11 \times 11 = 121$)
  - prime factors of 198 are **2, 3, 3, and 11** ($2 \times 3 \times 3 \times 11 = 198$)
  - prime factors of 264 are **2, 2, 2, 3, and 11** ($2 \times 2 \times 2 \times 3 \times 11 = 264$)

Odd, Even, Prime, and Composite Numbers

- Numbers can be grouped into a variety of categories, odd, even, prime, composite, positive, negative, and lots more
- **Odd numbers** include 1, 3, 5, 7, 9, 11, 13, 15, 17, 19, 21, and continue forever by adding 2 to the previous number
- **Even numbers** include 0, 2, 4, 6, 8, 10, 12, 14, 16, 18, 20, and continue forever by adding 2 to the previous number

---

- The next odd number can be found by adding or subtracting 2 from the current odd number or 1 to the current even number
- The next even number can be found by adding or subtracting 2 from the current even number or 1 to the current odd number
- Example, odd number 567, the next odd number larger than 567 is 567+2=569, and the next odd number smaller than 567 is 567-2=565

- In a similar manner, the next larger or smaller even number can be found by adding or subtracting 2 from the current even value
- A **PRIME NUMBER** is a number that can only be divided by itself or 1 without leaving a remainder or leaving a remainder of 0
- The first 15 prime numbers are, 2, 3, 5, 7, 11, 13, 17, 19, 23, 29, 31, 37, 41, 43, 47, and continue forever

		EVEN	ODD
ADDITION	EVEN	EVEN	ODD
SUBTRACTION	ODD	ODD	EVEN
MULTIPLICATION	EVEN	EVEN	EVEN
	ODD	EVEN	ODD

- There are many interesting characteristics about prime numbers   • For example, the number 2 is the only even prime number
- The number 5 is the only prime number ending in 5
- All prime numbers greater than 5 end in 1, 3, 7, or 9
- Another interesting feature of prime numbers is that there seems to be a a continuous supply of "twin prime" number pairs. A twin prime is a prime number with another prime number either +2 or −2 to the original prime number. Examples of the first few include, (3, 5), (5, 7), (11, 13), (17, 19), (29, 31), (41, 43), (59, 61), (71, 73), (101, 103), (107, 109), (137, 139), (149, 151), and so on
- See the appendix for more twin prime pairs

- Prime numbers are the prime factors of all composite numbers
- See the appendix at the end for a list of the first 75 composite numbers and their associated prime factors
- A **COMPOSITE number** is equal to the product of smaller prime numbers multiplied together
- The first few composite numbers are 4, 6, 8, 9, 10, 12, 14, 15, 16, 18, 20, 22, 24, 25, 26, 27, and 28
- The prime number factors of **4 = 2 * 2**. The prime number factors of **6 = 2 * 3**. The prime number factors of **8 = 2 * 2 * 2**, and the prime number factors of **10 = 2 * 5**
- See the appendix for the first 105 composite numbers and their associated prime factors

---

Factor, Factors, and Factoring

- **What is a Factor?**

- A factor is a nonzero integer whole number that <u>**divides**</u> the original number evenly without leaving a remainder or leaving a remainder of 0
- **Example, 17 is a factor of 51 since $51 \div 17 = 3$**
- **Example, 3 is also a factor of 51 since $51 \div 3 = 17$**
- Example, 2, 3, 6,7, 14, and 21 are all factor of 42 each of these factors can divide the number 42 evenly without leaving a remainder, however, only 2, 3, and 7 are the prime factors of 42 $2 \times 3 \times 7 = 42$

$42 \div 2 = 21$	$42 \div 3 = 14$	$42 \div 6 = 7$
$42 \div 7 = 6$	$42 \div 14 = 3$	$42 \div 21 = 2$

- **What are Factors?**
- Factors are nonzero integer whole numbers which, when <u>**multiplied together**</u> produce the original composite number.
- **Example, 17 and 3 are factors of 51 since 3×17**
- **Example, 2, 3, and 11 are factors of 66 since $2 \times 3 \times 11 =$**
- Example, what are the factors of 21? Since $3 \times 7 = 21$, the factors of 21 are 3 and 7. 3, and 7 are prime numbers, therefore, they are the <u>prime factors</u> of 21.
- Example, what are the factors of 30? Since $2 \times 15 = 30$, and $3 \times 10 = 30$, and $5 \times 6 = 30$, numbers 2, 3, 5, 6, 10, and 15 are all factors of 30
- The numbers 6, 10, and 15, are factors of 30, however, they are not the <u>prime factors</u> of 30 since each of these numbers has their own factors, $6 = 2 \times 3$, $10 = 2 \times 5$, and $15 = 3 \times 5$
- The <u>**prime factors**</u> of 30 therefore are 2, 3, and 5 since **$2 \times 3 \times 5 = 30$. The numbers 2, 3, and 5 are the smallest <u>prime numbers</u>** which when multiplied together equals 30
  - **Note, see prime number table in the appendix section**
  - **Note, Numbers 21 and 30 are composite numbers. They are products of other numbers.**

- **Factoring**

- **Example, Factoring the number 70**

- since 70 is an even number it can be evenly divided by 2
- 70 divided by prime number 2 = 35, and 35 divided by prime number 5 = 7, therefore numbers 2, 5, and 7, all prime number, are the prime factors of 70
  Check, $2 \times 5 \times 7 = 70$
  - Note, even numbers ending in 0, 2, 4, 6, or 8 can always be divided evenly by 2.
  - Note, numbers ending in 0 or 5 can always be evenly divided by 5.

- **Example, Factoring the number 104**
- Since 104 is an even number it can be evenly divided by 2, 104 divided by 2 = 52
- Since 52 is an even number it can also be evenly divided by 2, 52 divided by 2 = 26
- Since 26 is an even number it can be evenly divided by 2 as well, 26 divided by 2 = 13
- Since 13 is an odd number, ends in 3, and cannot be divided by any number other than itself, and 1 without leaving a remainder, it is a prime number. Therefore, 2, 4, 8, 13, 26, and 52 are all factors of 104, however, only numbers 2, 2, 2, and 13 are the prime factors of the number 104
- **Check, $2 \times 2 \times 2 \times 13 = 104$**

- **EXAMPLE**
- 108 is a composite number
- Factors of 108 are 2, 3, 4, 6, 9, 12, 18, 27, 36, and 54
- Prime factors of 108 are 2, 2, 3, 3, 3   • **check, $2 \times 2 \times 3 \times 3 \times 3 = 108$**

- **PRACTICE**
- Determine if the following numbers are composite numbers or prime numbers
- If the number is a composite find all the factors, identify the prime factors, and **check the results**

- 123 _____
- 195_____
- 322_____
- 579_____

- 152_____
- 221_____
- 396_____

- 177_____
- 271_____
- 428_____

Multiplying Fractions

- **Multiply the numerators together**
- **Multiply the denominators together**

- **EXAMPLES**

- $\left(\dfrac{3}{4} \times \dfrac{4}{5} \times \dfrac{5}{6}\right) = \dfrac{(3 \times 4 \times 5)}{(4 \times 5 \times 6)} = \dfrac{60}{120} = \left(\dfrac{60\,/\,60}{120\,/\,60}\right) = \dfrac{1}{2}$

- $\dfrac{13}{4} \times \dfrac{4}{7} = \dfrac{52}{28} = 1\dfrac{24}{28} = 1\left(\dfrac{24\,/\,4}{28\,/\,4}\right) = 1\dfrac{6}{7}$ **OR** $\left(\dfrac{52\,/\,4}{28\,/\,4}\right) = \dfrac{13}{7} = 1\dfrac{6}{7}$

- **EXAMPLE**

- $\dfrac{11}{17}\left(\dfrac{3}{4} \times \left(-\dfrac{4}{15}\right) \times \dfrac{7}{8}\right) = \dfrac{11}{17}\left(\dfrac{3}{4} \times \dfrac{-4}{15} \times \dfrac{7}{8}\right) = \dfrac{(11 \times 3 \times -4 \times 7)}{(17 \times 4 \times 15 \times 8)} = \dfrac{-924}{8160} = \left(\dfrac{-924\,/\,12}{8160\,/\,12}\right) = \dfrac{-77}{680}$

- Prime Factors of 77 are 7, and 11   • Prime factor of 680 are 2, 5, and 17
- Since there are no common factors, no further simplification is possible

---

- **PRACTICE**
- hint, convert all mixed numbers to improper fractions first
- Do the indicated operation and identify all prime factors
- (see example above)

- $\dfrac{9}{7} \times \left(\dfrac{-3}{4}\right) =$ _____   • $\dfrac{-7}{8} \times \left(-\dfrac{4}{9}\right) =$ _____   • $\left(\dfrac{12}{17}\right) \times \left(\dfrac{-3}{4}\right) \times \left(\dfrac{-5}{6}\right) =$ ____

- $\dfrac{-15}{17} \times -\dfrac{3}{5} \times \left(\dfrac{-34}{9}\right) \times \dfrac{2}{3} =$ ____   • $-\dfrac{11}{15} \times \left(4\dfrac{-1}{11}\right) =$ _____   • $\left(6\dfrac{-18}{9}\right) \times \left[3 - \dfrac{15}{27}\right] =$ _____

- $5\dfrac{-13}{17} \times \left[-7\dfrac{21}{31}\right] =$ _____   • $14\dfrac{1}{3} \times 13\dfrac{1}{4} =$ _____

Divide Fractions by Fractions

- To divide one fraction by another fraction MULTIPLY the fraction in the numerator by the **RECIPROCAL or INVERSE** of the fraction in the denominator.
- This is accomplished, in the example below, by multiplying the numerator N1 by the denominator **D2** and the denominator D1 by the numerator **N2**.

- **EXAMPLES**

$$\frac{N1}{D1} \div \frac{N2}{D2} = \frac{N1}{D1} \times \frac{D2}{N2} = \frac{(N1 \times D2)}{(D1 \times N2)} = \frac{N1D2}{N2D1}$$

$$\frac{1}{6} \div \frac{4}{9} = (1/6)/(4/9) = \frac{1}{6} \times \frac{9}{4} = \frac{(1 \times 9)}{(6 \times 4)} = \frac{9}{24} = \frac{(9/3)}{(24/3)} = \frac{3}{8}$$

prime factors for 3 = 1 × 3, prime factors for 8 = 2 × 2 × 2

no common factors

- $\frac{7}{11} \div \frac{5}{6} = \frac{7}{11} \times \frac{6}{5} = \frac{(7 \times 6)}{(11 \times 5)} = \frac{42}{55}$ **prime factors for 42 = 6 × 7**

- **prime factors for 55 = 5 × 11   no common factors**

- **PRACTICE**
- Do the indicated operation

- $\frac{3}{11} \div \frac{15}{22} =$ _____

- $4\frac{7}{8} \div 3\frac{9}{16} =$ _____

- $7\left(\frac{-3}{11}\right)/ -3\left(\frac{15}{22}\right) =$ _____

- $5/6\left(\frac{-15}{16}\right) =$ _____

- $\frac{1}{13} \div -\left(\frac{1}{39}\right) =$ _____

- $\frac{(7/11)}{(14/44)} =$ _____

- $\frac{1}{2} \div \left(\frac{2}{3} \div \frac{3}{4}\right) =$ _____

- $-9\frac{1}{13}/ -6\left(\frac{15}{16}\right) =$ _____

Divide Fractions by Whole Numbers

- 1st, CHANGE the (denominator) whole number to a fraction
- 2nd, MULTIPLY the (numerator, <u>top number</u>), fraction by the **RECIPROCAL** of the (denominator, <u>bottom number</u>) fraction
- In the example below, after multiplying the numerator by the **reciprocal** of the denominator, simplify the result expression by dividing both numerator and denominator by 2

- **EXAMPLES**

$$\frac{2}{3} \div 6 = \frac{2}{3} \div \frac{6}{1} = \frac{2}{3} \times \frac{1}{6} = \frac{2 \times 1}{3 \times 6} = \frac{2}{18} = \frac{2/2}{18/2} = \frac{1}{9}$$

- **Note,** $\frac{2/2}{18/2}$ **same as** $\dfrac{\frac{2}{2}}{\frac{18}{2}}$ **same as** $\frac{2}{2} / \frac{18}{2}$ **same as** $\frac{(2/2)}{(18/2)} = \frac{1}{9}$

- **PRACTICE**
- Preform the indicated operation
- Check the answer by multiplying the result by denominator

- $\frac{3}{11} \div 39 =$ _____

- $\frac{17}{4} \div 51 =$ _____

- $\frac{-53}{5} \div -106 =$ _____

- $\frac{11}{2} \div 99$ _____

- $\frac{617}{41} \div 1851 =$ _____

- $\frac{5}{17} \div -15 =$ _____

- $\frac{19}{23} \div -38 =$ _____

- $\frac{72}{-5} \div -216 =$ _____

- $\frac{-105}{3} \div 210 =$ _____

- $\frac{47}{-5} \div -235 =$ _____

Divide Whole Numbers by Fractions

- 1st Convert the (numerator) whole number to a fraction
- 2nd MULTIPLY the (numerator) now a fraction by the **RECIPROCAL** of the (denominator) fraction
- 3rd simplify the result
- In the example below, after multiplying the numerator by the **reciprocal** of the denominator, simplify the result expression by dividing both numerator and denominator by 3

- **EXAMPLES**

$$6 \div \frac{3}{8} = \left(\frac{6}{1} \div \frac{3}{8} \right) = \left(\frac{6}{1} \times \frac{8}{3} \right) = \frac{6 \times 8}{1 \times 3} = \frac{48 / 3}{3 / 3} = \frac{16}{1} = 16$$

- **PRACTICE**

- $11 \div \dfrac{21}{2} =$ _____

- $33 / (11 / 17) =$ _____

- $-9 \div \dfrac{3}{2}$ _____

- $18 / (-9 / 5) =$ _____

- $15 / \dfrac{5}{7} =$ _____

- $12 / \dfrac{6}{11} =$ _____

- $7 / \left(\frac{1}{3} \right) =$ _____

- $2 / \dfrac{1}{3} =$ _____

Divide Mixed Numbers by Whole Numbers

- Convert the (numerator) mixed number to an improper fraction
- Convert the (denominator) whole number to a fraction
- MULTIPLY the (numerator) fraction by the **RECIPROCAL** of the (denominator) fraction and simplify the results

---

- **EXAMPLE**

$$2\frac{5}{8} \div 3 = \frac{21}{8} \div \frac{3}{1} = \frac{21}{8} \times \frac{1}{3} = \frac{21 \times 1}{8 \times 3} = \frac{21}{24} = \frac{21/3}{24/3} = \frac{7}{8}$$

- **PRACTICE**

- $7\frac{3}{11} \div 13 = $ _____

- $12\frac{2}{15} \div 32 = $ _____

- $\left(5\frac{3}{16}\right) / 4 = $ _____

- $19\frac{3}{13} \div 26 = $ _____

- $3\frac{11}{19} \div 23 = $ _____

- $21\frac{31}{19} \div 29 = $ _____

- $8\left(\frac{2}{15}\right) / 32 = $ _____

Divide Whole Numbers
by Mixed Numbers

- Convert the (numerator) whole number to a fraction
- Convert the (denominator) mixed number to a fraction
- MULTIPLY the (numerator) fraction by the RECIPROCAL of the (denominator) fraction and simplify the results

---

- **EXAMPLE**

- $3 \div 2\dfrac{5}{8} = \dfrac{3}{1} \div \dfrac{21}{8} = \dfrac{3}{1} \times \dfrac{8}{21} = \dfrac{3 \times 8}{1 \times (3 \times 7)} = \dfrac{8}{7} = 1\dfrac{1}{7}$

- **PRACTICE**

- $12 \div 2\dfrac{4}{7} =$ _____

- $5 \div 3\dfrac{3}{16} =$ _____

- $11 \div 2\dfrac{4}{9} =$ _____

- $8 / \left(10\left(\dfrac{3}{4}\right)\right) =$ _____

- $9 \div 3\left(\dfrac{9}{11}\right) =$ _____

- $(1/2) / (1/3) / (1/4) =$ _____

- $49 / \left(4\dfrac{5}{11}\right) =$ _____

- $19 \div 5\dfrac{-1}{4} =$ _____

Divide Mixed Numbers by Fractions

- 1st Convert the (numerator) mixed number to an improper fraction
- 2nd MULTIPLY the (numerator) fraction by the RECIPROCAL of the (denominator) fraction and simplify the results

---

- **EXAMPLE**

- $2\dfrac{5}{8} \div \dfrac{7}{16} = \left(\dfrac{16}{8} + \dfrac{5}{8}\right) \div \dfrac{7}{16} = \dfrac{21}{8} \times \dfrac{16}{7} = \dfrac{3 \times 7 \times 2 \times 8}{8 \times 7} = \mathbf{6}$

- **PRACTICE**

- $11\dfrac{3}{7} \div \dfrac{5}{14} = $ _____

- $29\dfrac{7}{5} \div \dfrac{19}{11} = $ _____

- $11\dfrac{13}{17} \div \dfrac{19}{23} = $ _____

- $3\left(\dfrac{4}{-5}\right) \div \dfrac{6}{7} = $ _____

- $14\left(\dfrac{2}{7}\right) \div \dfrac{4}{17} = $ _____

- $7\left(\dfrac{2}{7}\right) \div \dfrac{5}{6} = $ _____

- $3\dfrac{3}{5} \div \dfrac{6}{7} = $ _____

- $4\dfrac{6}{-7} \div \dfrac{8}{9} = $ _____

Divide Fractions by Mixed Numbers

- 1st convert the denominator mixed number to an imperfect fraction
- 2nd multiply the numerator fraction by the RECIPROCAL or INVERSE of the denominator fraction and simplify the result
- This is accomplished, in the example below, by multiplying the numerator fraction, 5/9, by the reciprocal denominator fraction 18/55.

- **EXAMPLE**

- $\left(\dfrac{5}{9} \div 3\dfrac{1}{18} \right) = \dfrac{5}{9} \div \dfrac{55}{18} = \dfrac{5 \times 18}{9 \times 55} = \dfrac{18}{99} = \dfrac{2}{11}$

- **check,** $\left(\dfrac{2}{11} \times 3\dfrac{1}{18} \right) = \dfrac{2 \times \left((3 \times 18) + 1 \right)}{11 \times 18} = \dfrac{110}{198} = \dfrac{110/22}{198/22} = \dfrac{5}{9}$

- **PRACTICE**
- Preform the indicated operation
- Check the answer by multiplying the result by the denominator

- **Note,** $= 2\dfrac{3}{4} = 2 + \dfrac{3}{4} = \dfrac{11}{4}$ **however,** $2\left(\dfrac{3}{4} \right) = \left(\dfrac{2}{1} \times \dfrac{3}{4} \right) = \dfrac{2 \times 3}{1 \times 4} = \dfrac{6}{4} = 1\dfrac{1}{2}$

- **PRACTICE**

- $\dfrac{11}{12} \div 13\dfrac{14}{15} = $ _____

- $\dfrac{7}{11} \div 19\dfrac{17}{13} = $ _____

- $\dfrac{23}{31} \div 1\dfrac{5}{9} = $ _____

- $\dfrac{29}{11} \div 8\dfrac{11}{12} = $ _____

- $\dfrac{3}{2} \div 4\dfrac{5}{6} = $ _____

- $\dfrac{15}{7} \div 27\dfrac{9}{8} = $ _____

- $\dfrac{5}{9} \div 9\left(\dfrac{5}{11} \right) = $ _____

- $\dfrac{35}{42} \div 21\dfrac{22}{23} = $ _____

Divide Mixed Numbers by Mixed Numbers

- 1st Convert the (numerator) mixed number to an improper fraction
- 2nd Convert the (denominator) mixed number to an improper fraction
- 3rd MULTIPLY the (numerator) fraction by the RECIPROCAL of the (denominator) fraction and simplify the results

---

- **EXAMPLES**

$$\bullet\, 4\frac{7}{8} \div 5\frac{1}{5} = \frac{(32+7)}{8} \div \frac{(25+1)}{5} = \left(\frac{39}{8} \times \frac{5}{26}\right) = \frac{195}{208} = \frac{(195/13)}{(208/13)} = \frac{15}{16}$$

check, $\left(\dfrac{15}{16} \times 5\dfrac{1}{5}\right) = \dfrac{15 \times \left((5 \times 5) + 1\right)}{16 \times 5} = \dfrac{3 \times 5 \times 2 \times 13}{2 \times 8 \times 5} = \dfrac{39}{8} = 4\dfrac{7}{8}$

$$\bullet\, 9\frac{7}{11} \div 3\frac{29}{33} = \frac{(99+7)}{11} \div \frac{(99+29)}{33} = \left(\frac{106}{11} \times \frac{33}{128}\right) = \left(\frac{106 \times 33}{11 \times 128}\right) = \frac{(106 \times 33)/11}{(11 \times 128)/11} =$$

$$= \left(\frac{106 \times 3}{128}\right) = \frac{318}{128} = \frac{(318/2)}{(128/2)} = \frac{159}{64} = 2\frac{(159-128)}{64} = 2\frac{31}{64}$$

check, $\left(2\dfrac{31}{64} \times 3\dfrac{29}{33}\right) = \dfrac{(2 \times 64) + 31}{64} \times \dfrac{128}{33} = \dfrac{3 \times 53 \times 2 \times 64}{64 \times 3 \times 11} = \dfrac{106}{11} = 9\dfrac{7}{11}$

- **PRACTICE**
- Preform the indicated operation
- Check answer by multiplying the result by the mixed number in the denominator

- **Note,** $1\dfrac{2}{3} = \left(1 + \dfrac{2}{3}\right) = \dfrac{5}{3}$ **however,** $1\left(\dfrac{2}{3}\right) = \left(\dfrac{1}{1} \times \dfrac{2}{3}\right) = \dfrac{1 \times 2}{1 \times 3} = \dfrac{2}{3}$

- $9\dfrac{7}{8} \div 6\dfrac{4}{5} =$ _____

- $3\left(\dfrac{4}{5}\right) \div 6\left(\dfrac{7}{8}\right) =$ _____

- $5\left(\dfrac{5}{6}\right) \div 6\dfrac{6}{7} =$ _____

- $7\dfrac{8}{9} \div 10\left(\dfrac{11}{12}\right) =$ _____

- $23\dfrac{21}{31} \div 7\dfrac{9}{11} =$ _____

- $4\left(\dfrac{5}{6}\right) \div 7\left(\dfrac{8}{9}\right) =$ _____

- $6\dfrac{4}{5} \div 9\left(\dfrac{7}{8}\right) =$ _____

- $13\left(\dfrac{14}{15}\right) \div 16\dfrac{17}{18} =$ _____

Convert Decimals Numbers to Fractions

- Decimal numbers are numbers to the right of the decimal point

---

- **EXAMPLES,** 0.123, **and 0.098**, 123 and 098 are the decimal numbers
- The numerator of the new fraction is the number to the right of the decimal point including all zeros to the right of the decimal point and before the number digits.
- Example, **0.036** is decimal number we want to convert to a fraction. **036** is the number to the right of the decimal point and becomes the numerator of the new fraction. Notice in the examples below as soon as the denominator is determined the leading zeros in the numerator are discarded.
- The denominator of the new fraction is 1, followed by the number of zeros (0s) equal to the number of digit to the right of the decimal point including leading 0s.
- Ignore all trailing, rightmost zeros.

- **EXAMPLE**
- The numerator **036** has **3 digits**, the denominator is 1 followed by 3 zeros (1000) and the fraction is

$$= \frac{36}{1000} = \frac{36/4}{1000/4} = \frac{9}{250}$$

- **EXAMPLES**

$$0.002450 = \frac{00245}{100,000} = \frac{245}{100,000} = \frac{245/5}{100,000/5} = \frac{49}{20,000}$$

$$2.75000 = 2\frac{75}{100} = \frac{200}{100} + \frac{75}{100} = \frac{275}{100} = \frac{275/25}{100/25} = \frac{11}{4} = 2\frac{3}{4}$$

$$1.01250 = 1 + \frac{0125}{10000} = 1 + \frac{125/25}{10000/25} = 1 + \frac{5}{400} = 1 + \frac{5/5}{400/5} = 1 + \frac{1}{80}$$

$$3.62500 = 3 + \frac{625}{10000} = 3 + \frac{625/25}{10000/25} = 3 + \frac{25}{400} = 3 + \frac{25/25}{400/25} = 3\frac{1}{16}$$

- **PRACTICE**

- 2.240 = _____
- 0.03125 = _____
- 0.205 = _____
- 10.010 = _____

- 3.040 = _____
- 1.234 = _____
- 1.550 = _____
- 1.1000 = _____

- 4.025 = _____
- 0.010 = _____
- 0.602 = _____
- 2.220 = _____

Convert Fractions to Decimal (Long Division)

- Converting a fraction value (perfect, or imperfect fraction) to a decimal value requires dividing the numerator by the denominator
- **See Appendix A, B, and C for different Long Division Methods**
- If the value of the numerator is less than, or smaller than the value of the denominator, the value of the fraction is less than 1

- **EXAMPLE**

  $(3/8) < 1$ $(3/8) = 0.375$

- If the value of the numerator is greater, bigger, larger, or equal to the value of the denominator the value of the fraction is greater than or equal to 1

- **EXAMPLE**

  $(8/5) = 1\dfrac{3}{5} > 1$ $(8/5) = 1.6$

- To find the decimal equivalent of **3/8, (means 3 is divided by 8)**
- The denominator **8** must be divided into the numerator **3** using a calculator or by paper and pencil using long division
- The division process of dividing **3** by **8**, or dividing 8 into 3 means finding a **number**, which, when multiplied by **8** yields a result of **3**.
- The unknown decimal number is represented by **(D)** which is equal to the fraction **3/8**. This is expressed in the following equation **(D=3/8)**. Multiplying both side of this equation by 8 yields **8D = 8(3/8) = 3**
  - Note, multiplying both side of the equation by the same number does not change the value of the equation.
- So, **8D = 3** which means the value of **D** must be less than **1** to allow the product of **8 times D** to equal the value **3**. If D is set equal to 0.5, the value of 8D would be equal to 4, so, by quick observation we know D must be less than 0.5.

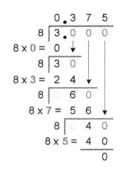

- **PRACTICE**

- $\dfrac{7}{16} = $ _____

- $\dfrac{3}{8} = $ _____

- $\dfrac{15}{7} = $ _____

- $3\dfrac{6}{7} = $ _____

- $\dfrac{13}{11} = $ _____

- $\dfrac{27}{72} = $ _____

- $\dfrac{21}{31} = $ _____

Finding the Square Root of a Fraction

- The square root of a fraction is the square root of the numerator divided by the square root of the denominator
- To find the square root of a fraction, ● **1st** find the square root of the numerator, ● **2nd** find the square root of denominator, ● **3rd** simplify the resulting fraction
- Note, the value of a fraction remains unchanged (does not change) if both numerator and denominator are multiplied or divided by the same value
- Only square roots with identical value inside the square root radical can be added and/or subtracted together

- **EXAMPLE**

$$2\sqrt{\frac{1}{4}} + 3\sqrt{\frac{1}{4}} = 5\sqrt{\frac{1}{4}} = 2.500$$

- **EXAMPLES**

$$\sqrt{\frac{a}{b}} = \frac{\sqrt{a}}{\sqrt{b}} \qquad \sqrt{\frac{1}{4}} = \frac{\sqrt{1}}{\sqrt{4}} = \frac{1}{2} \qquad \text{check } \frac{1}{2} \times \frac{1}{2} = \frac{1}{4} = 0.25$$

$$\sqrt{\frac{4}{16}} = \frac{\sqrt{4}}{\sqrt{16}} = \frac{2}{4} = \frac{(2/2)}{(4/2)} = \frac{1}{2} \quad OR = \sqrt{\frac{(4/4)}{(16/4)}} = \sqrt{\frac{1}{4}} = \frac{1}{2} = 0.500$$

$$\sqrt{\frac{80}{25}} = \sqrt{\frac{80/5}{25/5}} = \sqrt{\frac{16}{5}} = \frac{\sqrt{16}}{\sqrt{5}} = \frac{4}{\sqrt{5}} = \frac{4 \times \sqrt{5}}{\sqrt{5} \times \sqrt{5}} = \frac{4\sqrt{5}}{5} = 1.788 \ldots$$

  - Note, the square root of the fraction 80/25 can first be reduced before taking the square root
  - Note, the . . . following a decimal value indicates the number has been truncated, and there are additional decimal digits

---

- **PRACTICE**
- Simplify final answer with a whole number denominator
- Provide decimal equivalent of the result to at least 3 places (see examples above)

- $\sqrt{\dfrac{91}{26}} = $ _____

- $\sqrt{\dfrac{34}{85}} = $ _____

- $\sqrt{\dfrac{51}{68}} = $ _____

- $\sqrt{4\dfrac{5}{11}} = $ _____

- $\sqrt{6\left(\dfrac{102}{17}\right)} = $ _____

- $\sqrt{\dfrac{62}{93}} = $ _____

- $\sqrt{5\dfrac{1}{16}} + \sqrt{3\dfrac{5}{9}} = $ _____

- $\sqrt{7\dfrac{1}{9}} - \sqrt{5\dfrac{6}{15}} = $ _____

- $\sqrt{3\dfrac{5}{7}} / \sqrt{9\dfrac{11}{13}} = $ _____

What are EXPONENTS

- Exponent indicate how many times a number must be multiplied together by itself
- There are 2 parts to a number with an exponent, the <u>BASE</u> number and the <u>EXPONENT</u> number
- The lower number is the BASE number
- The upper number, placed above and to the right of the base number, is the EXPONENT number.
- Parentheses are typically used to group fraction elements together with the exponent place above and to the right of the right-most parentheses.

- **EXAMPLE**

$2^3 = 2 \times 2 \times 2 = 8$, Base = 2, Exponent = 3

- **EXAMPLE**

$$\left(\frac{2}{3}\right)^3 = \left(\frac{2}{3} \times \frac{2}{3} \times \frac{2}{3}\right) = \frac{2 \times 2 \times 2}{3 \times 3 \times 3} = \frac{8}{27}, \quad \text{Base} = \frac{2}{3}, \quad \text{exponent} = 3$$

- In text, exponents are indicated using the caret character (^)
- Example, 3^3 is the same as, $(3)^3 = 3 \times 3 \times 3 = 27$

- **EXAMPLES**

$$5^2 = 5^{(2)} = 5 \wedge 2 = 5^{+2} = 5^{(+2)} = 5 \times 5 = 25$$

$$\left(1/2\right)^2 = \left(1/2\right) \wedge 2 = (1/2) \times (1/2) = (1/4) = (0.5)^2 = 0.25$$

$$\left(3\frac{1}{4}\right)^2 = \left(\frac{13}{4}\right) \times \left(\frac{13}{4}\right) = \frac{169}{16} = 10 + \frac{9}{16} = 10\frac{9}{16} = 10.5625$$

- **Note, see Appendix D for alternative solution using $(a+b)^2$ method**

- Any fractions or number with an exponent can always be evaluated separately and independently obtaining a numeric result even if other operations are pending

- **EXAMPLE**

$$\left(\frac{1}{3}\right)^2 + 5^2 + \left(\frac{1}{2}\right)^3 = \frac{1}{3 \times 3} + 25 + \frac{1}{2 \times 2 \times 2} = \frac{1}{9} + 25 + \frac{1}{8} = 25\frac{17}{72}$$

Fractions and Numbers with Positive Exponents

- Fractions with exponents can be **ADDED** or **SUBTRACTED** together, by evaluating each fraction independently then add or subtract as indicated
- Alternatively, if the bases are the same, and the exponents are the same, the fractions can be initially combined, then apply the exponent
- In the example below, the exponent applies only to the fraction

---

- **EXAMPLE**

$$\left(\frac{1}{4}\right)^3 + \left(\frac{1}{4}\right)^3 = 2\left(\frac{1}{4}\right)^3 = 2\left(\frac{1}{64}\right) = \frac{1}{32}$$

- Fractions with the <u>same base</u>, but with <u>different or the same exponents</u> can be **MULTIPLIED** together by <u>ADDING</u> the exponent together

---

- **EXAMPLE**

$$\left(\frac{1}{3}\right)^2 \times \left(\frac{1}{3}\right)^3 = \left(\frac{1}{3}\right)^{(2+3)} = \left(\frac{1}{3}\right)^5 = \frac{1}{243}$$

- Fractions with **different bases**, and with the **same exponents**, can be **MULTIPLIED** together
  - <u>Multiply bases together first</u> then apply exponent

- **EXAMPLE**

$$\left(\frac{1}{3}\right)^3 \times \left(\frac{1}{4}\right)^3 = \left(\frac{1 \times 1}{3 \times 4}\right)^3 = \left(\frac{1}{12}\right)^3 = \frac{1}{12} \times \frac{1}{12} \times \frac{1}{12} = \frac{1}{1728}$$

- Alternatively, each fraction with its exponent, can be evaluated separately and independently

$$\left(\frac{1}{3}\right)^3 \times \left(\frac{1}{4}\right)^3 = \frac{1}{27} \times \frac{1}{64} = \frac{1}{1728}$$

- Fractions with <u>different bases</u> and <u>different exponents</u> can be MULTIPLIED together by evaluating each fraction separately then MULTIPLY the results together

---

• **EXAMPLE**

$$\left(\frac{3}{4}\right)^3 \times \left(\frac{2}{3}\right)^2 = \left(\frac{3}{4} \times \frac{3}{4} \times \frac{3}{4}\right) \times \left(\frac{2}{3} \times \frac{2}{3}\right) = \left(\frac{3}{4} \times \frac{3}{4} \times \frac{3}{4} \times \frac{2}{3} \times \frac{2}{3}\right) = \frac{3}{16}$$

• **PRACTICE**

• $\left(\dfrac{5}{7}\right)^3 = $ _____

• $\left(\dfrac{11}{9}\right)^3 = $ _____

• $5^3 - 3^4 = $ _____

• $(11)^3 = $ _____

• $(40)^3 = $ _____

• $(123 / 41)^3 = $ _____

• $(1.41421)^2 = $ _____

• $\sqrt{2} = $ _____

• $\left(\dfrac{7}{16}\right)^2 + \left(\dfrac{9}{16}\right)^3 = $ _____

• $(4^3)^2 = $ _____

• $\left(\dfrac{1}{2} + \left(\dfrac{1}{3}\right)^2\right)^3 = $ _____

Fractions and Numbers with Negative Exponents

- Fractions and numbers with negative exponents are first converted to an equivalent positive value and form, and then operated on as in previously examples

- **The general form for a negative exponent is** $a^{-x} = \dfrac{1}{a^x}$

- Fractions and numbers with negative exponents can be ADDED or SUBTRACTED together by evaluating each fraction independently then preform the addition or subtract as indicated

$$\left(\frac{3}{4}\right)^{-3} + \left(\frac{3}{4}\right)^{-3} = \left[\frac{1}{\left(\frac{3}{4}\right)^3} + \frac{1}{\left(\frac{3}{4}\right)^3}\right] = \frac{1}{\left(\frac{27}{64}\right)} + \frac{1}{\left(\frac{27}{64}\right)} = \left[\frac{\left(\frac{64}{27}\right)}{1} + \frac{\left(\frac{64}{27}\right)}{1}\right] =$$

$$= \frac{\left(\frac{128}{27}\right)}{1} = \frac{128}{27} = \left[\frac{108}{27} + \frac{20}{27}\right] = 4\frac{20}{27}$$

- Alternatively, if the bases are the same, and the exponents are the same, the fractions can be combined, and then the exponent is apply

$$\left(\frac{3}{4}\right)^{-3} + \left(\frac{3}{4}\right)^{-3} = 2\left[\frac{1}{\left(\frac{3}{4}\right)^3}\right] = \frac{2}{\frac{27}{64}} = 2\left(\frac{64}{27}\right) = \frac{128}{27} = 4\frac{128-108}{27} = 4\frac{20}{27}$$

- In the example below, the exponent applies only to the fraction

$$\left(\frac{1}{4}\right)^3 + \left(\frac{1}{4}\right)^3 = 2\left(\frac{1}{4}\right)^3 = 2\left(\frac{1}{64}\right) = \frac{2}{64} = \frac{1}{32}$$

- **EXAMPLE**

$$(1/2)^{-2} = \frac{1}{\left(\frac{1}{2}\right)^2} = \frac{1}{\left(\frac{1}{2} \times \frac{1}{2}\right)} = \frac{1}{\frac{(1\times 1)}{(2\times 2)}} = \frac{1}{\frac{1}{4}} = \frac{\left(\frac{1}{1} \times \frac{4}{1}\right)}{\left(\frac{1}{4} \times \frac{4}{1}\right)} = 4$$

$$4^{-3} = (4)^{-3} = 4^{(-3)} = (4)^{(-3)} = \frac{1}{4^3} = \frac{1}{4\times 4\times 4} = \frac{1}{64}$$

$$\left(3\frac{1}{4}\right)^{-2} = \left(\frac{13}{4}\right)^{-2} = \frac{1}{\left(\frac{13}{4}\right)^2} = \frac{1}{\left(\frac{13\times 13}{4\times 4}\right)} = \left[\frac{\frac{(4\times 4)}{(13\times 13)}}{1}\right] = \frac{16}{169}$$

$$\left(\frac{5}{11}\right)^{-3} = \frac{1}{\left(\frac{5}{11}\right)^3} = \frac{1}{\left(\frac{5}{11} \times \frac{5}{11} \times \frac{5}{11}\right)} = \frac{1}{\frac{125}{1331}} = \frac{\left(\frac{1}{1} \times \frac{1331}{27}\right)}{\left(\frac{125}{1331} \times \frac{1331}{125}\right)} = \frac{\frac{1331}{125}}{1} = 10\frac{(1331-1250)}{125} = 10\frac{81}{125}$$

- Fractions and numbers with negative exponents are first converted to an equivalent positive value and form, and then operated on
- Fractions and numbers with negative exponents can be **ADDED** or **SUBTRACTED** together by evaluating each fraction independently then preform the addition or subtract as indicated

---

- **EXAMPLE**

$$\left(\frac{3}{4}\right)^{-3} + \left(\frac{3}{4}\right)^{-3} = \frac{1}{\left(\frac{3}{4}\right)^3} + \frac{1}{\left(\frac{3}{4}\right)^3} = \left[\frac{1}{\frac{27}{64}} + \frac{1}{\frac{27}{64}}\right] = \frac{64}{27} + \frac{64}{27} = \frac{128}{27} =$$

$$= \frac{128}{27} = 4\frac{(128-108)}{27} = 4\frac{20}{27}$$

- **PRACTICE**

- $\left(\frac{1}{3}\right)^{-3} = $ _____

- $\left(\frac{5}{7}\right)^{-3} = $ _____

- $3\left(\frac{4}{5}\right)^{-4} = $ _____

- $13^{-2} = $ _____

- $\dfrac{(2^{-4})}{\left(\frac{1}{3}\right)} = $ _____

- $(7)^{-3} = $ _____

- $\left(\frac{1}{2}\right)^{-1} = $ _____

- $(1.41421)^{-2} = $ _____

- $2^{\left(\frac{1}{2}\right)} = $ _____

- $\left(\frac{3}{2}\right)^{-7}$ _____

- $\left(\frac{3}{4}\right)^{-3} \times \left(\frac{4}{3}\right)^{-4} = $ _____

- $\left(\frac{5}{9}\right)^{-2} = $ _____

- $\left(7\frac{1}{7}\right)^{-3} = $ _____

- $3\left(\frac{1}{5}\right)^{-4} = $ _____

Contrasting Positive and Negative Exponents

- general form for negative exponent

$$(\mathbf{a})^{-x} = \frac{1}{(\mathbf{a})^x}$$

- **EXAMPLES**

$2^5 = \dfrac{32}{1} = 32$

$2^9 = \dfrac{512}{1} = 512$

$3^4 = \dfrac{81}{1} = 81$

$3^5 = \dfrac{243}{1} = 243$

$(5)^2 = 25$

$\left(\dfrac{1}{2}\right)^2 = \left(\dfrac{1}{2} \times \dfrac{1}{2}\right) = \dfrac{1}{4}$

$\left(\dfrac{3}{7}\right)^3 = \dfrac{27}{343}$

$2^{-5} = \dfrac{1}{2^5} = \dfrac{1}{32} = 0.03125$

$2^{-9} = \dfrac{1}{512} = 0.001953125$

$3^{-4} = \dfrac{1}{3^4} = \dfrac{1}{81} = 0.0123456\ldots$

$3^{-5} = \dfrac{1}{243} = 0.0041152\ldots$

$(5)^{-2} = \dfrac{1}{(5)^2} = \dfrac{1}{25}$

$\left(\dfrac{1}{2}\right)^{-2} = \dfrac{1}{\left(\frac{1}{2}\right)^2} = \dfrac{1}{\left(\frac{1}{2} \times \frac{1}{2}\right)} = \dfrac{1}{\frac{1}{4}} = \dfrac{4}{1} = 4$

$\left(\dfrac{3}{7}\right)^{-3} = \dfrac{1}{\frac{27}{343}} = \dfrac{343}{27} = 12\dfrac{19}{27}$

Multiplying Fractions, Whole Numbers, Square Roots, Cube Roots, and nth Roots with Fractional Exponents

- Multiplying with <u>same Fractional Exponents</u>, multiply base

$$3^{\left(\frac{1}{2}\right)} \times 5^{\left(\frac{1}{2}\right)} = (3 \times 5)^{\left(\frac{1}{2}\right)} = \sqrt[2]{15}$$

- Multiplying with <u>same base</u>, add exponents

$$3^{\left(\frac{1}{2}\right)} \times 3^{\left(\frac{2}{3}\right)} = (3)^{\left(\frac{1}{2}+\frac{2}{3}\right)} = (3)^{\left(\frac{7}{6}\right)} = \sqrt[6]{(3)^7} = 3\sqrt[6]{3}$$

- Multiplying Numbers with <u>same base</u>, add exponents

$$(4)^3 \times (4)^4 = (4)^{(3+4)} = (4)^7$$

- Multiplying Square Roots, <u>same base</u>, add exponents

$$\left(\sqrt[2]{3}\right)^3 \times \left(\sqrt[2]{3}\right)^4 = \left(\sqrt[2]{3}\right)^{(3+4)} = \left(\sqrt[2]{3}\right)^7 = \sqrt[2]{3^{(3+4)}} = \sqrt[2]{3^7} = (3)^{\left(\frac{7}{2}\right)}$$

- **PRACTICE**

- $4^{\left(\frac{5}{6}\right)} \times 5^{\left(\frac{5}{6}\right)} = $ _____

- $\left(\dfrac{5}{6}\right)^{\left(\frac{3}{4}\right)} \times 2^{\left(\frac{3}{4}\right)} = $ _____

- $17^3 \times 17^4 = $ _____

- $\left(\dfrac{5}{6}\right)^{\left(\frac{3}{5}\right)} \times \left(\dfrac{5}{6}\right)^{\left(\frac{4}{5}\right)} = $ _____

- $11^{\left(\frac{5}{6}\right)} \times 11^{\left(\frac{3}{4}\right)} = $ _____

- $\left(\dfrac{5}{6}\right)^{\left(\frac{3}{4}\right)} \times \left(\dfrac{6}{5}\right)^{\left(\frac{4}{3}\right)} = $ _____

- $\left(\sqrt[2]{6}\right)^{\left(\frac{4}{5}\right)} \times \left(\sqrt[2]{6}\right)^{\left(\frac{3}{4}\right)} = $ _____

- $\left(\sqrt{\dfrac{2}{3}}\right)^{\left(\frac{5}{6}\right)} \times \left(\sqrt{\dfrac{2}{3}}\right)^{\left(\frac{3}{4}\right)} = $ _____

Fractions and Numbers with Positive Fractional Exponents

- The numerator of the fraction exponent is the power of the quantity
- The denominator of the fraction exponent is the root of the quantity

---

- **EXAMPLE**
- Find the cube root of 7 squared which means find a number when multiplied by itself 3 times is equal to **7^2 = 49**
- 3 cubed, **3^3=27** and **4^4=64,** the cube root of 49 is between 3 and 4

$$(7)^{\frac{2}{3}} = (7^2)^{\frac{1}{3}} = (49)^{\frac{1}{3}} = \left(\sqrt[3]{7}\right)^2 = \sqrt[3]{(7)^2} = \sqrt[3]{49} =$$

- Using the process described in Appendix D to find the cube root of 49 as follows:
- 1st estimate, 3.5, (3.5)^3 = 42.875, < 49, which means 42.875 <u>is less than</u> 49, so the next estimate must be increased
- 2nd estimate, 3.6, (3.6)^3 = 46.656 < 49, increase estimate
- 3rd estimate, 3.7, (3.7)^3 = 50.653 > 49, the estimate is now too large, the next estimate must be decrease
  - the cube root of 49 is now between 3.6 and 3.7, $3.6 < \sqrt[3]{49} < 3.7$
- 4th estimate, 3.65, and (3.65)^3 = 48.627125 < 49, increase estimate
  - the cube root of 49, **3.65 < 49 < 3.7**
- 5th estimate, 3.658, and (3.658)^3 = 48.947566312 < 49, increase estimate
  - the cube root of 49, **3.658 < 49 < 3.7**
- 6th estimate, 3.66, and (3.66)^3 = 49.027896 > 49, decrease estimate
  - the cube root of 49, **3.658 < 49 < 3.66**
- **calculator result** $= \sqrt[3]{49} = $ **3.6593057100229** . . .

- **EXAMPLE**
- find the **6th root** of **3/4** raised to the power of **5**

$$\left(\frac{3}{4}\right)^{\frac{5}{6}} = \sqrt[6]{\left(\frac{3}{4}\right)^5} = \frac{\sqrt[6]{3^5}}{\sqrt[6]{4^5}} = \frac{\sqrt[6]{243}}{\sqrt[6]{1024}} = \sqrt[6]{\frac{243}{1024}} =$$

$$= \sqrt[6]{\left(\frac{3}{4}\right)^5} = \sqrt[3]{\sqrt[2]{\left(\frac{3}{4}\right)^5}} = \sqrt[3]{\sqrt[2]{0.2373046875}} = \sqrt[3]{0.487139289628} \ldots$$

$$= \sqrt[6]{\left(\frac{3}{4}\right)^5} = \sqrt[3]{0.487139289628} \ldots = 0.786836297566 \ldots$$

- Above results are provided using a smart cell phone scientific calculator with both exponential and nth root functions.

- calculator result $= \left(\dfrac{3}{4}\right)^{\frac{5}{6}} = 0.786836297566\ldots$

- **EXAMPLE,** using the estimation process to find the 6th root of (3/4) raised to the 5th power by finding a number, which when multiplied by itself 6 times = (3/4) raised to the 5th power = 0.2373046875
- the process ---
- note, upe means increase the estimate, dne means decrease the estimate
- A quick visual examination of the problem helps us make the first estimate
- Since the exponent is almost 1, the solution is slightly more than 0.75
- 1st estimate 0.78, (0.78)^6 = 0.225199600704 < **0.2373046875**, upe
- 2nd estimate 0.79, (0.79)^6 = 0.43087455521 > **0.2373046875**, dne
- after 2 estimates the 6th root of **(3/4)^5**, is **0.78 < (3/4)^5 < 0.79**
- 3rd estimate 0.785, (0.785)^6 = 0.234001122366390625 < 0. **2373046875**, upe
- 4th estimate 0.786, (0.786)^6 = 0.235795371659574336 < 0. **2373046875**, upe
- 6th estimate (0.787)^6 = 0.237601071128220409 > 0. **2373046875**, dne
- after 6 estimates the 6th root of **(3/4)^5**, is **0.7865 < (3/4)^5 < 0.787**
- 7th estimate (0.7868)^6 = 0.237239012421331976065024 < 0. **2373046875**, upe
- after 7 estimates the 6th root of **(3/4)^5**, is **0.7868 < (3/4)^5 < 0.787**

- after 7 estimates $\quad \sqrt[6]{\left[\dfrac{3}{4}\right]^5} = 0.7868\ldots$

- calculator results $\quad \sqrt[6]{\left[\dfrac{3}{4}\right]^5} = 0.786836297566\ldots$

- **PRACTICE**

- $3^{\left(\frac{6}{5}\right)} =$ _____

- $\left(\dfrac{7}{8}\right)^{\frac{5}{4}} =$ _____

- $3\left(\dfrac{4}{5}\right)^{\left(\frac{6}{7}\right)} =$ _____

- $\left(2\dfrac{9}{16}\right)^{\frac{2}{3}} =$ _____

- $5\left(3\dfrac{4}{5}\right)^{\frac{2}{3}} =$ _____

- $\left(2\left(\dfrac{9}{16}\right)\right)^{\frac{2}{3}} =$ _____

- $\left(\dfrac{4}{9}\right)^{\left(\frac{2}{3}\right)} =$ _____

Fractions and Numbers with Negative Fractional Exponents

- The rule for negative exponents (fraction or whole number) is the value of a quantity (fraction, whole number, or other expression) with a negative exponent is always 1 divided by the quantity

- **general form for negative exponent**
$$(a)^{-x} = \frac{1}{(a)^{x}}$$

- The numerator of the fraction exponent is the power and indicates how many times the quantity is multiplied by itself
- The denominator of the fraction exponent is the root of the quantity raised to the numerator of the fraction exponent

- **EXAMPLE**
- calculate 7 raised to the power of (-2/3)
- Since the exponent is negative the quantity is moved to the denominator with a 1 in the numerator

$$(7)^{\left(\frac{-2}{3}\right)} = \left[\left(7^{2}\right)^{-\left(\frac{1}{3}\right)}\right] = \frac{1}{\sqrt[3]{7^{2}}} = \frac{1}{\sqrt[3]{49}} = \frac{1}{3.6593\ldots} = 0.27327\ldots$$

hint – reduce to that of a single number, and a single operation

- $\left(\frac{\cdot}{9}\right)$ = _____

Word Problems with Fraction

- A **12 foot** flag pole is extended an additional **1/3** of its present length.
- How long is the new flag pole?

- My friend has a fish pond in his back yard which is 10 feet long, 5 feet wide and 4 feet deep
- The volume of the fish pond is 10 **ft** × 5 **ft** × 4 **ft** = 200 **cuft**
- There is a total of **7.4805** gallons of water in each cubic foot.
- How many gallons of water in the fish pond if it filled only **3/4 full?**
- How many gallons of water in the fish pond if it filled **7/8 full?**

- Show how $5 / 8 \div 3 / 4 = 5 / 6$

- Four sevenths of the 5th grade class of 28 students are girls and five thirteenths of 26 students in the 6th grade class are girls.
- How many girls in the 5th and 6th grades classes combined?
- How many boys in the 6th grade class?

- Show that $\sqrt[4]{\left(2\right)^5} = \left[\sqrt[4]{2}\right]^5$

- A family drove 3125 miles coast to coast across the US. The car broke down twice, first at 572 miles and again at 3072 miles.
- What is the fraction of mile driven between breakdowns compared to the total trip miles?

Appendix A - Original and Formal Method for Manual Solution of Long Division Problems

- The manual method is the most common and formal (paper and pencil) method of solving long division problems.
- Each digit or digit group of the dividend is **compared, by subtraction,** to the next **single digit, or digit group quotient trial estimate, multiplied by the divisor**.

- The dividend can be extended by adding as many zeros (0s) to the right side of the dividend to increase the resolution of the result and continue the process. The decimal point is placed in the quotient directly above its location in the dividend.
  - Note, adding 0s to the right side of a number, and to the right of the decimal point does not change the value. Adding 0s to the left side of a number, left of the decimal point does not change the value.

- Each trial digit (working left to right) is multiplied by the divisor and subtracted from the previous remainder. The example at the right depicts the details of 7 divided by 16.
- The numerator (7) is the dividend, the denominator (16) is the divisor, and the decimal result (0.4375) is the quotient, and the answer.
- The leftmost digit of the dividend is evaluated first. Since it is less than the divisor (7<16), a 0 is placed above the first digit.
- A comparison is performed by subtracting the (**divisor quotient product**) from the dividend, 7-(16*0) = 7. A zero (0) is then appended to the 7, making it **70**
  - Note, the 4 red zeros in the picture are the appended zeros.

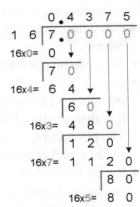

Since the dividend, 7, is less than the divisor, 16, the quotient (the answer) is less than 1

- The new dividend is **70**, it is greater than the divisor (**70 > 16**), the estimate is at least 4 times larger and the process repeats. Multiplication, then subtraction, **70-(16*4) = 70-64 = 6.**
  The estimate **4** is placed above the appended zero.
- The process continues until the entire dividend is process in a similar manner. The last subtraction may produce a remainder, a value other than 0, but less than the divisor. Any number of zeros (0s) may be appended at the right of the dividend to increase the resolution as necessary.

Appendix B - Sum of Multipliers Method for Manual Solution of Long Division Problems

- Another relatively simple method for solving long division problems is the sum of divisor or denominator products. Estimates are multiplied by the divisor
- The product result is subtracted from the dividend, or numerator, and repeated until the final difference is less than the divisor or 0.

- **EXAMPLE, 500 divided by 3**
- A convenient estimate is made (100) is selected, such that 3 times the estimate is less than (500)
- The product of the divisor and the estimate is (300)
- The product is then subtracted from the original dividend (500) leaving a remainder of (200)
- Since the remainder is greater than the dividend, the process repeats
- Next estimate is (60), product is (180), and the remainder is (20)
- Since (20) > (3) the process continues, the next estimate is (6), product is (18), remainder is (2). • Since the remainder now is less than the dividend, the process ends.
- The product factors (100, 60, 6) and the remainder (2) are all added together to produce the final result, 166 and 2/3
- Result is checked by multiplying the final result with the divisor and comparing the result to the original dividend

- **EXAMPLE, 26,917 divided by 1727**
- This example ends with a large value remainder which is simplified for best answer then checked by multiplying the final result with the divisor and comparing the result to the original dividend.

Sum Of Multipliers Long Division

```
          3 | 5 0 0
    1 0 0 | 3 0 0
          |  2 0 0
      6 0 | 1 8 0
          |   0 2 0
        6 |     1 8
  ─────────────────
    1 6 6 |     0 2
```

$$= 166 \frac{2}{3}$$

Check, $3 \times (166 + (2/3)) =$
$498 + (6/3) = 498 + 2 = 500$

Sum Of Multipliers Long Division

```
  1 7 2 7 | 2 6 9 1 7
    1 0 | 1 7 2 7 0
        |  0 9 6 4 7
      5 |     8 6 3 5
  ──────────────────────
    1 5 |     1 0 1 2
```

$$= 15 \frac{1012}{1727} = 15 \frac{11 \times 92}{11 \times 157} = 15 \frac{92}{157}$$

Check, $1727 \times (15 + (92/157)) =$
$25,905 + (158,884/157) =$
$25,905 + 1012 = 26,917$

Appendix C - Successive Approximation, or Successive Estimation Method for Manual Solution of Long Division, Exponentiation, Square Root, and nth Root Problems

- The successive approximation manual method for solving long division problems requires only multiplication followed by analysis of the product result for the next estimate
- The accuracy of the result increases with each iteration.
- This process requires an initial approximation, an estimate, or even a simple guess as to what the final answer might be.
- The closer the initial estimate is to the final answer the fewer the number of calculations it takes to arrive at an acceptable final answer.

- **EXAMPLE, 34,567 divided by 89, (34,457 is the dividend, 89 is the divisor).** ● For this example, **89** times the final answer **(the quotient)** is equal to **34,567,** and in equation form, $X = 34{,}567 / 89$, $89X = 34{,}567$.
- We can see that the result will (most likely) be a 3digit number because the product of a 2digit number multiplied by a 3digit number, will (most of the time) result in a $(2 + 3 = 5)$ 5digit number.
- The smallest 3digit number is 100, and if used as the initial estimate $(89 \times 100 = 8900)$ it would work, however, it is significantly too small for a good first estimate. ● By observation, a number 4 times larger would be a better choice. Since $(89 \times 400 = 35{,}600)$ is a value much closer to the **34,567** dividend, **400** is selected as the first estimate.
- The next steps are just continuously repeated until a final result is determined. The process can terminate anytime the answer produces sufficient accuracy and resolution.
- estimate $400 \times 89 = 35{,}600$ is larger than 34,567, reduce next estimate
- estimate $390 \times 89 = 34{,}710$ is larger than 34,567, reduce next estimate
- estimate $380 \times 89 = 33{,}820$ is smaller than 34,567, increase next estimate
- **Answer is now between 380 and 390**
- Estimate $385 \times 89 = 34{,}265$ is smaller than 34,567, increase next estimate
- Estimate $387.5 \times 89 = 34{,}487.5$ is smaller than 34,567, increase next estimate
- Estimate $89 \times 388.625 = 34{,}587.625$ is larger than 34,567, reduce next estimate
  - **Answer is between 387.5 and 388.625**
- Estimate $388.5 \times 89 = 34{,}576.5$ is larger than 34,567, reduce next estimate
- Estimate $388.4 \times 89 = 34{,}567.6$ is larger than 34,567, reduce next estimate
- Estimate $388.39 \times 89 = 34{,}566.71$ is smaller than 34,567, increase next estimate

- **Answer is between 388.39 and 388.4**
- Estimate **388.395 × 89 = 34,567.155** is larger than 34,567, reduce next estimate
  - **Answer is between 388.39 and 388.395**
- Estimate **388.394 × 89 = 34,567.066** is larger than 34,567, reduce next estimate
- Estimate **388.393 × 89 = 34,566.977** smaller than 34,567, increase next estimate
  - **Answer is now between 388.393 and 388.394**
- Estimate **388.3935 × 89 = 34,567.0215** is larger than 34,567, reduce next estimate
  - **Answer is now between 388.393 and 388.3935**
- Estimate **388.3932 × 89 = 34,566.9948** is smaller than 34,567, increase next est.
- Answer is now between 388.3932 and 388.3935
  - **Calculator result is 388.393,258,426,966,292 . . . .**
- The Successive Approximation Method can be directly applied to finding Square Roots and solving nth Root problems.

- **EXAMPLE,** using a fraction exponent, where the numerator of the fraction is the power, and the denominator of the fraction is the root, this example expresses the 5th root of 23 cubed

$$23^{\left(\frac{3}{5}\right)} = \sqrt[5]{(23)^3} = \sqrt[5]{(23 \times 23 \times 23)} = \sqrt[5]{12,167} =$$

- 1st estimate is 10 $10^5 = 100,000 > 12,167$
- 2nd estimate is 5 $5^5 = 3125 < 12,167$
- 3rd estimate is 7 $7^5 = 16.807 > 12,167$
- 4th estimate is 6.5 $(6.5)^5 = 11,602.90625 < 12,167$
- 5th estimate is 6.55 $(6.55)^5 = (6.55)^2 \times (6.55)^2 \times (6.55) = (6.55)^{(2+2+1)} =$
  $= 42.9025 \times 42.9025 \times 6.55 = 12,056.0905159375 < 12,167$
- 6th estimate is 6.56 $(6.56)^5 = 12,148.4031819776 < 12,167$
- 7th estimate is 6.57 $(6.57)^5 = 12,241.2804495057 > 12,167$
- 8th estimate is 6.561 $(6.561)^5 = 12,157.665459056928801 < 12,167$
- 9th estimate is 6.5615 $(6.5615)^5 = 12,162.29871565671005759375 < 12,167$
- 10th estimate is 6.5619 $(6.5619)^5 = 12,166.00633789983970164099 < 12,167$
- 11th estimate is 6.562 $(6.562)^5 = 2,166.933384727052832 < 12,167$
- 12th estimate is 6.56205 $(6.562)^5 = 12,167.39692933240014921006 28125 > 12,167$

$$6.562 < 23^{\left(\frac{3}{5}\right)} = \sqrt[5]{12,167} < 6.56205$$

- **Calculator result, 5th root of 23×23x23 = 6.562007185515855 . . .**
- The example above illustrates the successive estimation method and the associated process
- The 5th estimate above, **estimate 6.55,** demonstrates and explains how a 4 function calculator can be used to calculate numbers with exponents. In this example, 3 multiplications are required to calculate (6.55)^5.
- Additional estimates can continue to resolve the result to more and more decimal places if needed
- It is recognized that although the process is a little tedious, only multiplication is needed to resolve the answer to any accuracy, and since only multiplication is needed a 4function calculator or pencil and paper is adequate to solve these types of problems

Appendix D – Solution for $(a + b)^2$

- Solution using $(a + b)^2$ method for solving $\left(3\frac{1}{4}\right)^2$

- $(a + b)^2 = (a \times a) + (2 \times a \times b) + (b \times b) =$

  $= a^2 + 2ab + b^2$

- $\left(3\frac{1}{4}\right)^2 = \left(3 + \frac{1}{4}\right) \times \left(3 + \frac{1}{4}\right) = (3 \times 3) + 2 \times \left(3 \times \frac{1}{4}\right) + \left(\frac{1}{4} \times \frac{1}{4}\right) =$

- $= 9 + \frac{6}{4} + \frac{1}{16} = 9 + \frac{24 + 1}{16} = 9\frac{25}{16} = 9 + 1\frac{9}{16} = 10\frac{9}{16} =$

  $= 10.5625$

- Check, show that $\left(10\frac{9}{16}\right) / \left(3\frac{1}{4}\right) = 3\frac{1}{4}$

  $\left(10\frac{9}{16}\right) / \left(3\frac{1}{4}\right) = \left(\frac{169}{16}\right) \times \left(\frac{4}{13}\right) = \frac{13 \times 13 \times 4}{13 \times 4 \times 4} = \frac{13}{4} = 3\frac{1}{4}$

Appendix D - Multiplication Table

	1	2	3	4	5	6	7	8	9	10	11	12	13	14	15	16
1	1	2	3	4	5	6	7	8	9	10	11	12	13	14	15	16
2	2	4	6	8	10	12	14	16	18	20	22	24	26	28	30	32
3	3	6	9	12	15	18	21	24	27	30	33	36	39	42	45	48
4	4	8	12	16	20	24	28	32	36	40	44	48	52	56	60	64
5	5	10	15	20	25	30	35	40	45	50	55	60	65	70	75	80
6	6	12	18	24	30	36	42	48	54	60	66	72	78	84	90	96
7	7	14	21	28	35	42	49	56	63	70	77	84	91	98	105	112
8	8	16	24	32	40	48	56	64	72	80	88	96	104	112	120	128
9	9	18	27	36	45	54	63	72	81	90	99	108	117	126	135	144
10	10	20	30	40	50	60	70	80	90	100	110	120	130	140	150	160
11	11	22	33	44	55	66	77	88	99	110	121	132	143	154	165	176
12	12	24	36	48	60	72	84	96	108	120	132	144	156	168	180	192
13	13	26	39	52	65	78	91	104	117	130	143	156	169	182	195	208
14	14	28	42	56	70	84	98	112	126	140	154	168	182	196	210	224
15	15	30	45	60	75	90	105	120	135	150	165	180	195	210	225	240
16	16	32	48	64	80	96	112	128	144	160	176	192	208	224	240	256
17	17	34	51	68	85	102	119	136	153	170	187	204	221	238	255	272
18	18	36	54	72	90	108	126	144	162	180	198	216	234	252	270	288
19	19	38	57	76	95	114	133	152	171	190	209	228	247	266	285	304
20	20	40	60	80	100	120	140	160	180	200	220	240	260	280	300	320

- Note – The numbers with gray background are perfect squares. The square roots of these numbers are the horizontal and vertical 1 through 16 index numbers.

	17	18	19	20	21	22	23	24	25	26	27	28	29	30	31	32
17	289	306	323	340	357	374	391	408	425	442	459	476	493	510	527	544
18	306	324	342	360	378	396	414	432	450	468	486	504	522	540	558	576
19	323	342	361	380	399	418	437	456	475	494	513	532	551	570	589	608
20	340	360	380	400	420	440	460	480	500	520	540	560	580	600	620	640
21	357	378	399	420	441	462	483	504	525	546	567	588	609	630	651	672
22	374	396	418	440	462	484	506	528	550	572	594	616	638	660	682	704
23	391	414	437	460	483	506	529	552	575	598	621	644	667	720	744	768
24	408	432	456	480	504	528	552	576	600	624	648	672	696	720	744	768
25	425	450	475	500	525	550	575	600	625	650	675	700	725	750	775	800
26	442	468	494	520	546	572	598	624	650	676	702	728	754	780	806	832
27	459	486	513	540	567	594	621	648	675	702	729	756	783	810	837	864
28	476	504	532	560	588	616	644	672	700	728	756	784	812	840	868	896
29	493	522	551	580	609	638	667	696	725	754	783	812	841	870	899	928
30	510	540	570	600	630	660	690	720	750	780	810	840	870	900	930	960
31	527	558	589	620	651	682	713	744	775	806	837	868	899	930	961	992
32	544	576	608	640	672	704	736	768	800	832	864	896	928	960	992	1024

Appendix E - Scientific Notation and Powers of 10

- Scientific Notation is a shorthand method of writing numbers. It can be used to write numbers which are very large and numbers which are very small
- For example, the distance from the earth to the sun is approximately 92 million miles, 92,000,000 miles = 92×10^{6} miles = 9.2×10^{7} miles = **$9.2 \times 10,000,000$ miles**
- The diameter of 1 atom is between 0.1 nm and 0.5 nm. (1 nm is 1 nanometer which is 1×10^{-9} meters.) The diameter of 1 atom is between 1×10^{-10} and 5×10^{10} meters.
- Scientific Notation has 3 parts, the coefficient (the number), the base, and the exponent. The 1st part is the number, a value greater than or equal to 1 and less than 10. The 2nd part is the base. For all the examples on this page the base is 10. The 3rd part is the exponent.

- **EXAMPLES**
- 15 million = 15,000,000 = 15×10^{6}
- 1 inch = 25.4 mm = 2.54 centimeters = $2.54 \ 10^{-2}$ meters
- 1 millimeter = 1 mm = 0.03937… inches = $3.937… \times 10^{-2}$ inches
- Equatorial Diameter of the earth is 7.926×10^{3} miles, 1.275×10^{4} km
- Polar Diameter of the earth is 7.89986×10^{3} miles, 1.2713×10^{4} km

$1 = 1^{0}$	$1.0 = 1^{0} = 1/1$
$10 = 10^{1}$	$0.1 = 10^{-1} = 1/10$
$100 = 10^{2}$	$0.01 = 10^{-2} = 1/100$
$1000 = 10^{3}$	$0.001 = 10^{-3} = 1/1000$

- **Multiplication** when the bases are the same
  - multiply the coefficients together
  - add the exponents together
  - adjust both exponent and coefficient if the coefficient is greater than 10 or less than 1

- **EXAMPLE,** $(4.5 \times 10^{3}) * (6.7 \times 10^{2}) = 30.15 \times 10^{5} = 3.015 \times 10^{6}$
- **Addition** when exponents are the same
  - add coefficients together
  - If the coefficient after addition is greater than 10 adjust both exponent and coefficient

- **Addition** when exponents are not the same
  - adjust the exponents to be the same by adjusting both exponents and coefficient
  - adjust both coefficient and exponent as necessary to allow the value to remain the same
  - add the coefficients together
  - adjust both exponent and coefficient if the coefficient is greater than 10 or less than 1

- **EXAMPLE**
- $(4.5 \times 10^{\wedge}3) + (6.7 \times 10^{\wedge}2) = (4.5 \times 10^{\wedge}3) + (0.67 \times 10^{\wedge}3) = 5.17 \times 10^{\wedge}3$

$1.0 = 1 \times 10^0$ $1.0 = 1 \times 10^0 = 1/1$

$10.0 = 1 \times 10^1$ $0.10 = 1 \times 10^{-1} = 1/10$

$100.0 = 1 \times 10^2$ $0.010 = 1 \times 10^{-2} = 1/100$

$1000.0 = 1 \times 10^3$ $0.0010 = 1 \times 10^{-3} = 1/1000$

$9,800,000,000 = 9.8 \times 10^9$

$7,654,321 = 7.654321 \times 10^6$

$560,000 = 5.6 \times 10^5$

$1,234 = 1.234 \times 10^3$

$678 = 6.78 \times 10^2$

$0.987 = 9.87 \times 10^{-1}$

$0.034 = 3.4 \times 10^{-2}$

$0.000056 = 5.6 \times 10^{-5}$

$0.0000000098 = 9.8 \times 10^{-9}$

Appendix F - First 1000 Prime Numbers (2 through 7917)

2	3	5	7	11	13	17	19	23	29	31	37	41	43	47	53	59	61	67	71
73	79	83	89	97	101	103	107	109	113	127	131	137	139	149	151	157	163	167	173
179	181	191	193	197	199	211	223	227	229	233	239	241	251	257	263	269	271	277	281
283	293	307	311	313	317	331	337	347	349	353	359	367	373	379	383	389	397	401	409
419	421	431	433	439	443	449	457	461	463	467	479	487	491	499	503	509	521	523	541
547	557	563	569	571	577	587	593	599	601	607	613	617	619	631	641	643	647	653	659
661	673	677	683	691	701	709	719	727	733	739	743	751	757	761	769	773	787	797	809
811	821	823	827	829	839	853	857	859	863	877	881	883	887	907	911	919	929	937	941
947	953	967	971	977	983	991	997	1009	1013	1019	1021	1031	1033	1039	1049	1051	1061	1063	1069
1087	1091	1093	1097	1103	1109	1117	1123	1129	1151	1153	1163	1171	1181	1187	1193	1201	1213	1217	1223
1229	1231	1237	1249	1259	1277	1279	1283	1289	1291	1297	1301	1303	1307	1319	1321	1327	1361	1367	1373
1381	1399	1409	1423	1427	1429	1433	1439	1447	1451	1453	1459	1471	1481	1483	1487	1489	1493	1499	1511
1523	1531	1543	1549	1553	1559	1567	1571	1579	1583	1597	1601	1607	1609	1613	1619	1621	1627	1637	1657
1663	1667	1669	1693	1697	1699	1709	1721	1723	1733	1741	1747	1753	1759	1777	1783	1787	1789	1801	1811
1823	1831	1847	1861	1867	1871	1873	1877	1879	1889	1901	1907	1913	1931	1933	1949	1951	1973	1979	1987
1993	1997	1999	2003	2011	2017	2027	2029	2039	2053	2063	2069	2081	2083	2087	2089	2099	2111	2113	2129
2131	2137	2141	2143	2153	2161	2179	2203	2207	2213	2221	2237	2239	2243	2251	2267	2269	2273	2281	2287
2293	2297	2309	2311	2333	2339	2341	2347	2351	2357	2371	2377	2381	2383	2389	2393	2399	2411	2417	2423
2437	2441	2447	2459	2467	2473	2477	2503	2521	2531	2539	2543	2549	2551	2557	2579	2591	2593	2609	2617
2621	2633	2647	2657	2659	2663	2671	2677	2683	2687	2689	2693	2699	2707	2711	2713	2719	2729	2731	2741
2749	2753	2767	2777	2789	2791	2797	2801	2803	2819	2833	2837	2843	2851	2857	2861	2879	2887	2897	2903
2909	2917	2927	2939	2953	2957	2963	2969	2971	2999	3001	3011	3019	3023	3037	3041	3049	3061	3067	3079
3083	3089	3109	3119	3121	3137	3163	3167	3169	3181	3187	3191	3203	3209	3217	3221	3229	3251	3253	3257
3259	3271	3299	3301	3307	3313	3319	3323	3329	3331	3343	3347	3359	3361	3371	3373	3389	3391	3407	3413
3433	3449	3457	3461	3463	3467	3469	3491	3499	3511	3517	3527	3529	3533	3539	3541	3547	3557	3559	3571
3581	3583	3593	3607	3613	3617	3623	3631	3637	3643	3659	3671	3673	3677	3691	3697	3701	3709	3719	3727
3733	3739	3761	3767	3769	3779	3793	3797	3803	3821	3823	3833	3847	3851	3853	3863	3877	3881	3889	3907
3911	3917	3919	3923	3929	3931	3943	3947	3967	3989	4001	4003	4007	4013	4019	4021	4027	4049	4051	4057
4073	4079	4091	4093	4099	4111	4127	4129	4133	4139	4153	4157	4159	4177	4201	4211	4217	4219	4229	4231
4241	4243	4253	4259	4261	4271	4273	4283	4289	4297	4327	4337	4339	4349	4357	4363	4373	4391	4397	4409
4421	4423	4441	4447	4451	4457	4463	4481	4483	4493	4507	4513	4517	4519	4523	4547	4549	4561	4567	4583
4591	4597	4603	4621	4637	4639	4643	4649	4651	4657	4663	4673	4679	4691	4703	4721	4723	4729	4733	4751
4759	4783	4787	4789	4793	4799	4801	4813	4817	4831	4861	4871	4877	4889	4903	4909	4919	4931	4933	4937
4943	4951	4957	4967	4969	4973	4987	4993	4999	5003	5009	5011	5021	5023	5039	5051	5059	5077	5081	5087
5099	5101	5107	5113	5119	5147	5153	5167	5171	5179	5189	5197	5209	5227	5231	5233	5237	5261	5273	5279
5281	5297	5303	5309	5323	5333	5347	5351	5381	5387	5393	5399	5407	5413	5417	5419	5431	5437	5441	5443
5449	5471	5477	5479	5483	5501	5503	5507	5519	5521	5527	5531	5557	5563	5569	5573	5581	5591	5623	5639
5641	5647	5651	5653	5657	5659	5669	5683	5689	5693	5701	5711	5717	5737	5741	5743	5749	5779	5783	5791
5801	5807	5813	5821	5827	5839	5843	5849	5851	5857	5861	5867	5869	5879	5881	5897	5903	5923	5927	5939
5953	5981	5987	6007	6011	6029	6037	6043	6047	6053	6067	6073	6079	6089	6091	6101	6113	6121	6131	6133
6143	6151	6163	6173	6197	6199	6203	6211	6217	6221	6229	6247	6257	6263	6269	6271	6277	6287	6299	6301
6311	6317	6323	6329	6337	6343	6353	6359	6361	6367	6373	6379	6389	6397	6421	6427	6449	6451	6469	6473
6481	6491	6521	6529	6547	6551	6553	6563	6569	6571	6577	6581	6599	6607	6619	6637	6653	6659	6661	6673
6679	6689	6691	6701	6703	6709	6719	6733	6737	6761	6763	6779	6781	6791	6793	6803	6823	6827	6829	6833
6841	6857	6863	6869	6871	6883	6899	6907	6911	6917	6947	6949	6959	6961	6967	6971	6977	6983	6991	6997
7001	7013	7019	7027	7039	7043	7057	7069	7079	7103	7109	7121	7127	7129	7151	7159	7177	7187	7193	7207
7211	7213	7219	7229	7237	7243	7247	7253	7283	7297	7307	7309	7321	7331	7333	7349	7351	7369	7393	7411
7417	7433	7451	7457	7459	7477	7481	7487	7489	7499	7507	7517	7523	7529	7537	7541	7547	7549	7559	7561
7573	7577	7583	7589	7591	7603	7607	7621	7639	7643	7649	7669	7673	7681	7687	7691	7699	7703	7717	7723
7727	7741	7753	7757	7759	7789	7793	7817	7823	7829	7841	7853	7867	7873	7877	7879	7883	7901	7907	7919

Appendix G - First 105 Composite Numbers (4 through 141) and associated Prime Factors

Number							
4	2	2					
6	2	3					
8	2	2	2				
9	3	3					
10	2	5					
12	2	2	3				
14	2	7					
15	3	5					
16	2	2	2	2			
18	2	3	3				
20	2	2	5				
21	3	7					
22	2	11					
24	2	2	2	3			
25	5	5					
26	2	13					
27	3	3	3				
28	2	2	7				
30	2	3	5				
32	2	2	2	2	2		
33	3	11					
34	2	17					
35	5	7					
36	2	2	3	3			
38	2	19					
39	3	13					
40	2	2	2	5			
42	2	3	7				
44	2	2	11				
45	3	3	5				
46	2	23					
48	2	2	2	2	3		
49	7	7					
50	2	5	5				
51	3	17					

Number							
52	2	2	13				
54	2	3	3	3			
55	5	11					
56	2	2	2	7			
57	3	19					
60	2	2	3	5			
62	2	31					
63	3	3	7				
64	2	2	2	2	2	2	
65	5	13					
66	2	3	11				
68	2	2	17				
69	3	23					
70	2	5	7				
72	2	2	2	3	3		
74	2	37					
75	3	5	5				
76	2	2	19				
77	7	11					
78	2	3	13				
80	2	2	2	2	5		
81	3	3	3	3			
82	2	41					
84	2	2	3	7			
85	5	17					
86	2	43					
87	3	29					
88	2	2	2	11			
90	2	3	3	5			
91	7	13					
92	2	2	23				
93	3	31					
94	2	47					
95	5	19					
96	2	2	2	2	2	3	

Number							
98	2	7	7				
99	3	3	11				
100	2	2	5	5			
102	2	3	17				
104	2	2	2	13			
105	3	5	7				
106	2	53					
108	2	2	3	3	3		
110	2	3	17				
111	3	37					
112	2	2	2	2	7		
114	2	3	19				
115	5	23					
116	2	2	29				
117	3	3	13				
118	2	59					
119	7	17					
120	2	2	2	3	5		
121	11	11					
122	2	61					
123	3	41					
124	2	2	31				
125	5	5	5				
126	2	3	3	7			
128	2	2	2	2	2	2	2
129	3	43					
130	2	5	13				
132	2	2	3	11			
133	7	19					
134	2	67					
135	3	3	3	5			
136	2	2	2	17			
138	2	3	23				
140	2	2	5	7			
141	3	47					

Appendix H - Numbers in Different Bases (16, 10, 8, 5, 3, and 2)

BASE					
16	10	8	5	3	2
Hexadecimal	Tens	Octal	fives	Tertiary	Binary
14	20	24	40	202	10100
13	19	23	34	201	10011
12	18	22	33	200	10010
11	17	21	32	122	10001
10	16	20	31	121	10000
F	15	17	30	120	1111
E	14	16	24	112	1110
D	13	15	23	111	1101
C	12	14	22	110	1100
B	11	13	21	102	1011
A	10	12	20	101	1010
9	9	11	14	100	1001
8	8	10	13	22	1000
7	7	7	12	21	111
6	6	6	11	20	110
5	5	5	10	12	101
4	4	4	4	11	100
3	3	3	3	10	11
2	2	2	2	2	10
1	1	1	1	1	1
0	0	0	0	0	0

Appendix J – Answers

- **Adding and Subtracting Signed Whole Numbers, page 7**

  - $9 + 18 = +27$
  - $21 - 19 = +2$
  - $-4 - (-9) = -5$
  - $-(-7) + (-29) = -22$

  - $7 - 16 = -9$
  - $-18 + 5 = -13$
  - $+11 - 12 = -1$
  - $(-9 + 27) = +18$

  - $3 + 14 = +11$
  - $-3 - 11 = -14$
  - $-3 + (-14) = -17$
  - $-(-3) + (-19) = -16$

  - $-8 - 9 = -17$
  - $-3 + 14 = +11$
  - $+4 + 5 = +9$
  - $4 - (+7) = -3$

- **Multiplying and Dividing Signed Whole Numbers, page 8**

  - $17 \times 3 = 51$
  - $-39 / -3 = +13$

  - $(-12) / -3 = -4$
  - $-42 / (-(-6)) = -7$

  - $-27 / 9 = -3$
  - $+54 / -9 = -6$

  - $9 \times 4 = 36$
  - $78 / -13 = -6$

  - $-13(-7 + 23) / 19 = -\dfrac{13(16)}{19} = \dfrac{-208}{19} = -\left(\dfrac{190 + 18}{19}\right) = -10 + \dfrac{18}{19} = -10\dfrac{18}{19}$

  - $+129 / -43 = -3$
  - $-91 / +13 = -7$
  - $-84 \div -6 = 14$

  - $(+(-46)) / (-(+23)) = 2$
  - $(45 + 9) / (-9) = +(54 / -9) = -6$

  - $78 / -(13 \times -3) = 78 / -(-39) = 2$
  - $5(-23) \div -(-46) = 2\dfrac{1}{2} = -2.5$

  - $-19 \times 7 / 76 = -133 \div 76 = -1 + ((133 - 76) / 76) = -1 + (57 / 76) = -1 + \left(\dfrac{3 \times 19}{4 \times 19}\right) = -1\dfrac{3}{4}$

- **Change Improper Fractions to Mixed Numbers, page 10**

  - $\dfrac{23}{7} = 3\dfrac{2}{7}$
  - $\dfrac{28}{17} = 1\dfrac{11}{17}$
  - $\dfrac{37}{19} = 1\dfrac{18}{19}$

  - $\dfrac{7}{4} = 1\dfrac{3}{4}$
  - $\dfrac{11}{4} = 2\dfrac{3}{4}$
  - $\dfrac{29}{9} = 3\dfrac{2}{9}$

  - $\dfrac{19}{5} = 3\dfrac{4}{5}$
  - $\dfrac{33}{8} = 4\dfrac{1}{8}$
  - $\dfrac{43}{6} = 7\dfrac{1}{6}$

  - $\dfrac{29}{11} = 2\dfrac{7}{11}$
  - $\dfrac{18}{16} = 1\dfrac{1}{8}$
  - $\dfrac{23}{12} = 1\dfrac{11}{12}$

- **Change Mixed Numbers to Improper Fractions, page 11**

  - $2\dfrac{4}{5} = \dfrac{14}{5}$
  - $22\dfrac{1}{3} = \dfrac{67}{3}$

  - $3\dfrac{7}{8} = \dfrac{31}{8}$
  - $31\dfrac{1}{4} = \dfrac{125}{4}$

  - $9\dfrac{2}{3} = \dfrac{29}{3}$
  - $5\dfrac{6}{7} = \dfrac{41}{7}$

  - $11\dfrac{9}{11} = \dfrac{130}{11}$
  - $11\dfrac{3}{4} = \dfrac{47}{4}$

- **Change Mixed Numbers to Improper Fractions, page 11**

- $9\dfrac{7}{16} = \dfrac{151}{16}$ • $6\dfrac{6}{5} = \dfrac{36}{5}$ • $8\dfrac{13}{7} = \dfrac{69}{7}$ • $17\dfrac{11}{3} = \dfrac{62}{3}$

- $13\dfrac{3}{8} = \dfrac{107}{8}$ • $9\dfrac{1}{6} = \dfrac{55}{6}$ • $7\dfrac{2}{9} = \dfrac{65}{9}$

- **Adding and Subtracting Fractions with Same Denominators, page 12**

- $\dfrac{11}{7} - \dfrac{5}{7} = +\dfrac{6}{7} = \dfrac{+6}{7}$ • $\dfrac{13}{17} + \dfrac{3}{17} = +\dfrac{16}{17}$ • $\dfrac{4}{21} + \dfrac{13}{21} = +\dfrac{17}{21} = \dfrac{17}{21}$

- $\dfrac{7}{19} - \dfrac{13}{19} = \dfrac{-6}{19} = -\dfrac{6}{19}$ • $\dfrac{-3}{8} - \dfrac{5}{8} = -1$ • $\dfrac{13}{15} + \dfrac{-4}{15} = \dfrac{2}{3}$

- $\dfrac{4}{13} - \dfrac{+3}{13} = \dfrac{7}{13}$ • $\dfrac{-9}{14} - \dfrac{-3}{14} = \dfrac{-6}{7}$

- **Adding and Subtracting Fractions with Different Denominators, page 13**

- $\dfrac{5}{6} - \dfrac{3}{4} = \dfrac{1}{12}$ • $\dfrac{5}{8} + \dfrac{7}{12} = 1\dfrac{5}{24}$ • $\dfrac{11}{18} - \left(\dfrac{-5}{6}\right) = 1\dfrac{4}{9}$ • $\dfrac{-13}{17} + \dfrac{-6}{34} = -\dfrac{16}{17}$

- $-\dfrac{11}{12} + \left(\dfrac{-3}{4}\right) = -1\dfrac{2}{3}$ • $\dfrac{-18}{9} - \dfrac{-10}{27} = -1\dfrac{5}{9}$ • $\dfrac{13}{21} + \dfrac{5}{7} = 1\dfrac{1}{3}$ • $\dfrac{11}{6} - \dfrac{3}{4} = 1\dfrac{1}{12}$

- **Factor, Factors, and Factoring, page 19**

  - 123 is composite • 152 is composite • 177 is composite • 195 is composite • 221 is composite
  - 271 is prime • 322 is composite • 396 is composite • 428 is composite • 579 is composite

- **Multiplying Fractions, page 20**

• $\dfrac{9}{7} \times \left(\dfrac{-3}{4}\right) = -\dfrac{27}{28}$	• Prime Factors of 27 are 3, 3, and 3 • Prime Factors of 28 are 2, 2, and 7
• $\dfrac{-7}{8} \times \left(-\dfrac{4}{9}\right) = \dfrac{7}{18}$	• Prime Factors of 7 are 7 and 1 • Prime Factors of 18 are 2, 3, and 3
• $\left(\dfrac{12}{17}\right) \times \left(\dfrac{-3}{4}\right) \times \left(\dfrac{-5}{6}\right) = \dfrac{15}{34}$	• Prime Factors of 15 are 3, and 5 • Prime Factors of 34 are 2, and 17
• $\dfrac{-15}{17} \times -\dfrac{3}{5} \times \left(\dfrac{-34}{9}\right) \times \dfrac{2}{3} = -2$	• Prime Factors of 2 are 2, and 1 • Prime Factors of 3 are 3, and 1
• $-\dfrac{11}{15} \times \left(4\dfrac{-1}{11}\right) = \dfrac{4}{15}$	• Prime Factors of 4 are 2, and 2 • Prime Factors of 15 are 3, and 5

- $\left(6\dfrac{-18}{9}\right) \times \left[3 - \dfrac{15}{27}\right] = 9\dfrac{7}{9}$

  - Prime Factors of 7 are 1, and 7
  - Prime Factors of 9 are 3, and 3

- $\left(5\dfrac{-13}{17}\right) \times \left[-7\dfrac{21}{31}\right] = -32\dfrac{16}{31}$

  - Prime Factors of 16 are 2, 2, 2, and 2
  - Prime Factors of 31 are 1, and 31

- $14\dfrac{1}{3} \times 13\dfrac{1}{4} = \dfrac{2279}{12}$

  - Prime Factors of 2279 are 43, and 53
  - Prime Factors of 12 are 2, 2, and 3

- **Divide Fractions by Fractions, page 21**

- $\dfrac{3}{11} \div \dfrac{15}{22} = \dfrac{(2)}{(5)}$

  - Prime Factors of 2 are 1, and 2
  - Prime Factors of 5 are 1, and 5

- $\dfrac{1}{13} \div -\left(\dfrac{1}{39}\right) = -3$

  - Prime Factors of 3 are 1, and 3

- $4\dfrac{7}{8} \div 3\dfrac{9}{16} = 1\dfrac{7}{19}$

  - Prime Factors of 7 are 1, and 7
  - Prime Factors of 19 are 1, and 19

- $\left(\dfrac{7\,/\,11}{14\,/\,44}\right) = 2$

  - Prime Factors of 2 are 1, and 2

- $7\left(\dfrac{-3}{11}\right) / -3\left(\dfrac{15}{22}\right) = \dfrac{14}{15}$

  - Prime Factors of 14 are 2, and 7
  - Prime Factors of 15 are 3, and 5

- $-9\dfrac{1}{12} / -6\left(\dfrac{15}{16}\right) = 1\dfrac{83}{135}$

  - Prime Factors of 83 are 1, and 83
  - Prime Factors of 135 are 3, 3, 3, and 5

- $\dfrac{1}{2} \div \left(\dfrac{2}{3} \div \dfrac{3}{4}\right) = \dfrac{9}{16}$

  - Prime Factors of 9 are 3, and 3
  - Prime Factors of 16 are 2, 2, 2, and 2

- $5\,/\,6\left(\dfrac{-15}{16}\right) = -\dfrac{8}{9}$

  - Prime Factors of 8 are 2, 2, and 2
  - Prime Factors of 9 are 3, and 3

- **Divide Fractions by Whole Numbers, page 22**

- $\dfrac{3}{11} \div 39 = \dfrac{1}{143}$

- $\dfrac{5}{17} \div -15 = -\dfrac{1}{51}$

- $\dfrac{17}{4} \div 51 = \dfrac{1}{12}$

- $\dfrac{19}{23} \div -38 = -\dfrac{1}{46}$

- $\dfrac{-53}{5} \div -106 = \dfrac{1}{10}$

- $\dfrac{72}{-5} \div -216 = \dfrac{1}{15}$

- $\dfrac{11}{2} \div 99 = -\dfrac{1}{46}$

- $\dfrac{-105}{3} \div 210 = -\dfrac{1}{6}$

- $\dfrac{617}{41} \div 1851 = -\dfrac{1}{46}$

- $\dfrac{47}{-5} \div -235 = -\dfrac{1}{46}$

- **Divide Whole Numbers by Fractions, page 23**

- $11 \div \dfrac{21}{2} = 1\dfrac{1}{21}$

- $15 / \dfrac{5}{7} = 21$

- $33 / (11 / 17) = 51$

- $12 / \dfrac{6}{11} = 22$

- $-9 \div \dfrac{3}{2} = -6$

- $\dfrac{7}{(1/3)} = 21$

- $18 / (-9 / 5) = -10$

- $2 / \dfrac{1}{3} = 6$

- **Divide Mixed Numbers by Whole Numbers, page 24**

- $7\dfrac{3}{11} \div 14 = \dfrac{40}{77}$

- $3\dfrac{11}{19} \div 23 = \dfrac{68}{437}$

- $12\dfrac{2}{15} \div 32 = \dfrac{91}{240}$

- $21\dfrac{31}{19} \div 29 = \dfrac{220}{551}$

- $\left(5\dfrac{5}{16}\right) / 5 = 1\dfrac{1}{16}$

- $8\left(\tfrac{2}{15}\right) / 32 = \dfrac{1}{30}$

- $19\dfrac{3}{13} \div 26 = \dfrac{125}{169}$

- **Divide Whole Numbers by Mixed Numbers, page 25**

- $12 \div 2\dfrac{4}{7} = \dfrac{14}{3} = 4\dfrac{2}{3}$

- $9 \div 3\left(\dfrac{9}{11}\right) = 3 + \dfrac{2}{3} = 3\dfrac{2}{3}$

- $5 \div 3\dfrac{3}{16} = \dfrac{11}{6} = 1\dfrac{5}{6}$

- $1 / 2 / 1 / 3 / 1 / 4 = \dfrac{12}{2} = 6$

- Directions of operations for multiply, divide, addition, and subtract are left to right

- General solution $\quad 1 / \mathbf{a} / 1 / \mathbf{b} / 1 / \mathbf{c} / 1 / \mathbf{d} = \left(\dfrac{1}{\mathbf{a}}\right) \times \left(\dfrac{\mathbf{b}}{1}\right) \times \left(\dfrac{\mathbf{c}}{1}\right) \times \left(\dfrac{\mathbf{d}}{1}\right)$

- INCORRECT

- $1 / 2 / (1 / 3) / 1 / 4 = \left(\dfrac{1}{2}\right) / \left(\dfrac{1}{3} \times \dfrac{4}{1}\right) = \left(\dfrac{1}{2}\right) / \left(\dfrac{4}{3}\right) = \left(\dfrac{1}{2} \times \dfrac{3}{4}\right) = \dfrac{3}{8}$

- $11 \div 2\dfrac{4}{9} = \dfrac{11}{1} \div \left(\dfrac{18}{9} + \dfrac{4}{9}\right) = \dfrac{11}{1} \times \left(\dfrac{9}{22}\right) = \dfrac{11 \times 9}{11 \times 2} = \dfrac{9}{2} = 4\dfrac{1}{9}$

- $49 / \left(4\dfrac{5}{11}\right) = \dfrac{49}{1} \div \left(\dfrac{44}{11} + \dfrac{5}{11}\right) = \left(\dfrac{49}{1} \div \dfrac{49}{11}\right) = \dfrac{49}{1} \times \left(\dfrac{11}{49}\right) = \dfrac{49 \times 11}{1 \times 49} = \dfrac{11}{1} = 11$

- $8 / \left(10\left(\dfrac{3}{4}\right)\right) = \dfrac{8}{1} \div \dfrac{10 \times 3}{4} = \dfrac{8}{1} \times \dfrac{4}{30} = \dfrac{8 \times 4}{1 \times 30} = \dfrac{2 \times 16}{2 \times 15} = \dfrac{16}{15} = 1\dfrac{1}{15}$

- $19 \div 5\dfrac{-1}{4} = \dfrac{19}{1} \div \left(\dfrac{40}{8} - \dfrac{1}{4}\right) = \dfrac{19}{1} \div \left(\dfrac{40}{8} - \dfrac{2}{8}\right) = \dfrac{19}{1} \times \left(\dfrac{8}{38}\right) = \dfrac{19 \times 8}{1 \times 2 \times 19} = 4$

- **Divide Mixed Numbers by Fractions, page 26**

- $11\dfrac{3}{7} \div \dfrac{5}{14} = 32$

- $14\left(\dfrac{2}{7}\right) \div \dfrac{4}{17} = 17$

- $29\dfrac{7}{5} \div \dfrac{19}{11} = 17\dfrac{3}{5}$

- $7\left(\dfrac{2}{7}\right) \div \dfrac{5}{6} = 2\dfrac{2}{5}$

- $11\dfrac{13}{17} \div \dfrac{19}{23} = 14\dfrac{78}{323}$

- $3\dfrac{3}{5} \div \dfrac{6}{7} = 4\dfrac{1}{5}$

- $3\left(\dfrac{4}{-5}\right) \div \dfrac{6}{7} = -2\dfrac{4}{5}$

- $4\dfrac{6}{-7} \div \dfrac{8}{9} = 3\dfrac{15}{28}$

- **Divide Fractions by Mixed Numbers, page 27**

- $\dfrac{11}{12} \div 13\dfrac{14}{15} = \dfrac{5}{76}$

- $\dfrac{7}{11} \div 19\dfrac{17}{13} = \dfrac{91}{2904}$

- $\dfrac{23}{31} \div 1\dfrac{5}{9} = \dfrac{207}{434}$

- $\dfrac{29}{11} \div 8\dfrac{11}{12} = \dfrac{348}{1177}$

- $\dfrac{3}{2} \div 4\dfrac{5}{6} = \dfrac{9}{29}$

- $\dfrac{15}{7} \div 27\dfrac{9}{8} = \dfrac{8}{105}$

- $\dfrac{5}{9} \div 9\left(\dfrac{5}{11}\right) = \dfrac{11}{81}$

- $\dfrac{35}{42} \div 21\dfrac{22}{23} = \dfrac{23}{606}$

- **Divide Mixed Numbers by Mixed Numbers, page 28**

- $9\dfrac{7}{8} \div 6\dfrac{4}{5} = 1\dfrac{123}{272}$

- $23\dfrac{21}{31} \div 7\dfrac{9}{11} = 3\dfrac{38}{1333}$

- $3\left(\dfrac{4}{5}\right) \div 6\left(\dfrac{7}{8}\right) = \dfrac{16}{35}$

- $4\left(\dfrac{5}{6}\right) \div 7\left(\dfrac{8}{9}\right) = \dfrac{15}{28}$

- $5\left(\dfrac{5}{6}\right) \div 6\dfrac{6}{7} = \dfrac{175}{288}$

- $6\dfrac{4}{5} \div 9\left(\dfrac{7}{8}\right) = \dfrac{272}{315}$

- $7\dfrac{8}{9} \div 10\left(\dfrac{11}{12}\right) = \dfrac{142}{165}$

- $13\left(\dfrac{14}{15}\right) \div 16\dfrac{17}{18} = \dfrac{1092}{1525}$

- **Convert Decimals to Fractions, page 29**

- $2.240 = \dfrac{56}{25} = 2\dfrac{6}{25}$

- $3.040 = \dfrac{76}{25} = 3\dfrac{1}{25}$

- $4.025 = \dfrac{161}{40} = 4\dfrac{1}{40}$

- $0.03125 = \dfrac{1}{32}$

- $1.234 = \dfrac{617}{500} = 1\dfrac{117}{500}$

- $0.010 = \dfrac{1}{100}$

- $0.205 = \dfrac{41}{200}$

- $1.550 = \dfrac{31}{20} = 1\dfrac{11}{20}$

- $0.602 = \dfrac{301}{500} \approx \dfrac{3}{5}$

- $10.010 = \dfrac{1001}{100} = 10\dfrac{1}{100}$

- $1.1000 = \dfrac{11}{10} = 1\dfrac{1}{10}$

- $2.220 = \dfrac{111}{50} = 2\dfrac{11}{50}$

- **Convert Fractions to Decimals, page 30**

- $\dfrac{7}{16} = 0.4375$

- $\dfrac{3}{8} = 0.375$

- $\dfrac{15}{7} = 2.1428$, **with a remainder of** 4

- $\dfrac{15}{7} = 2.142857\ldots$

- $3\dfrac{6}{7} = \dfrac{27}{7} = 3.8571428\ldots$

- $\dfrac{13}{11} = 1.181818$ **with a remainder of** 9, **also** $1,18181818\ldots$

- $\dfrac{13}{11} = 1.8181818\ldots$

- $\dfrac{27}{72} = 0.375$

- $\dfrac{21}{31} = 0.677419$, **with a remainder of** 11

- $\dfrac{21}{31} = 0.677419\ldots$

- **Finding the Square Root of a Fraction, page 31**

- $\sqrt{\dfrac{91}{26}} = \dfrac{1}{2}\sqrt{14} = 1.8708\ldots$

- $\sqrt{\dfrac{34}{85}} = \dfrac{1}{5}\sqrt{10} = 0.6324555\ldots$

- $\sqrt{\dfrac{51}{68}} = \dfrac{1}{2}\sqrt{3} = 0.8660254\ldots$

- $\sqrt{4\dfrac{5}{11}} = \dfrac{7}{11}\sqrt{11} = 2.11057\ldots$

- **Finding the Square Root of a Fraction, page 31, continued**

- $\sqrt{6\left(\dfrac{102}{17}\right)} = \sqrt{36} = 6.000$

- $\sqrt{\dfrac{62}{93}} = \dfrac{1}{3}\sqrt{6} = 0.81649\ldots$

- $\sqrt{\dfrac{62}{93}} = \sqrt{\dfrac{2}{3}} = \sqrt[2]{\dfrac{2}{3}} = \sqrt{0.66666\ldots} = 0.81649\ldots$

- $\sqrt{5\dfrac{1}{16}} + \sqrt{3\dfrac{5}{9}} = 2.250 + 1.885618\ldots = 4.135618\ldots$

- $\sqrt{7\dfrac{1}{9}} - \sqrt{5\dfrac{6}{15}} = 0.3429\ldots$

- $\sqrt{3\dfrac{5}{7}} \,/\, \sqrt{9\dfrac{11}{13}} = \dfrac{13\sqrt{7}}{56} = 0.6141922\ldots$

- **Fractions and Numbers with Positive Exponents, page 34**

- $\left(\dfrac{5}{7}\right)^3 = \dfrac{125}{343} = 0.364401\ldots$

- $\left(\dfrac{5}{7}\right)^3 = (0.7142857\ldots)^3 = 0.364422\ldots$

- $\left(\dfrac{11}{9}\right)^3 = 1.825788\ldots$

- $\left(\dfrac{11}{9}\right)^3 = (1.22222\ldots)^3 = 1.82577\ldots$

- $5^3 - 3^4 = 44$
- $(40)^3 = 64{,}000$
- $(1.41421)^2 = 1.9999899\ldots$
- $\left(\dfrac{7}{16}\right)^2 + \left(\dfrac{9}{16}\right)^3 = \dfrac{1513}{4096} = \dfrac{17(89)}{2^{12}}$
- $\left(\dfrac{1}{2} + \left(\dfrac{1}{3}\right)^2\right)^3 = \dfrac{1331}{5832} = 0.228969\ldots$

- $(11)^3 = 1331$
- $(123\,/\,41)^3 = 27$
- $\sqrt{2} = 1.41421\ldots$
- $\left(4^3\right)^2 = 2^{12} = 4096$

• **Fractions and Numbers with Negative Exponents, page 36**

• $\left(\dfrac{1}{3}\right)^{-3} = 27$

• $\left(\dfrac{5}{7}\right)^{-3} = 2\dfrac{93}{125}$

• $3\left(\dfrac{4}{5}\right)^{-4} = 7\dfrac{83}{125}$

• $13^{-2} = \dfrac{1}{169}$

• $\dfrac{(2^{-4})}{\left(\frac{1}{3}\right)} = \dfrac{3}{16}$

• $7^{-3} = \dfrac{1}{343}$

• $\left(\dfrac{1}{2}\right)^{-1} = 2$

• $(1.41421)^{-2} \approx \dfrac{1}{2}$

• $2^{\left(\frac{1}{2}\right)} \approx 1.41421\ldots$

• $\left(\dfrac{3}{2}\right)^{-7} = \dfrac{128}{2187}$

• $\left[\left(\dfrac{3}{4}\right)^{-3} \times \left(\dfrac{4}{3}\right)^{-4}\right] = 0.75$

• $\left(\dfrac{5}{9}\right)^{-2} = 3.24$

• $\left(7\dfrac{1}{7}\right)^{-3} = 0.00274\ldots$

• $3\left(\dfrac{1}{5}\right)^{-4} = 1875$

• **Multiplying Fractions, Whole Numbers, Square Roots, Cube Roots, and nth Roots with Fractional Exponents, page 38**

• $4^{\left(\frac{5}{6}\right)} \times 5^{\left(\frac{5}{6}\right)} = 12.139244\ldots$

• $\left(\dfrac{5}{6}\right)^{\left(\frac{3}{4}\right)} \times 2^{\left(\frac{3}{4}\right)} = 1.466852\ldots$

• $17^3 \times 17^4 = 410{,}338{,}673$

• $\left(\dfrac{5}{6}\right)^{\left(\frac{3}{5}\right)} \times \left(\dfrac{5}{6}\right)^{\left(\frac{4}{5}\right)} = 0.774722\ldots$

• $11^{\left(\frac{5}{6}\right)} \times 11^{\left(\frac{3}{4}\right)} = 44.552466\ldots$

• $\left(\dfrac{5}{6}\right)^{\left(\frac{3}{4}\right)} \times \left(\dfrac{6}{5}\right)^{\left(\frac{4}{3}\right)} = 1.11221434\ldots$

• $\left(\sqrt[2]{6}\right)^{\left(\frac{4}{5}\right)} \times \left(\sqrt[2]{6}\right)^{\left(\frac{3}{4}\right)} = 4.00928767\ldots$

• $\left[\sqrt{\dfrac{2}{3}}\right]^{\left(\frac{5}{6}\right)} \times \left[\sqrt{\dfrac{2}{3}}\right]^{\left(\frac{3}{4}\right)} = 0.5262460388\ldots$

• **Fractions and Numbers with Positive Fractional Exponents, page 40**

• $3^{\left(\frac{6}{5}\right)} = 3.73719\ldots$

• $\left(\dfrac{7}{8}\right)^{\frac{5}{4}} = 0.84627\ldots$

• $3\left(\dfrac{4}{5}\right)^{\left(\frac{6}{7}\right)} = 2.4777388\ldots$

• $\left(2\dfrac{9}{16}\right)^{\frac{2}{3}} = 1.872590\ldots$

- $5\left(3\frac{4}{5}\right)^{\frac{2}{3}} = 12.17565\ldots$

- $\left(2\left(\frac{9}{16}\right)\right)^{\frac{2}{3}} = 1.08168\ldots$

- $\left(\frac{4}{9}\right)^{\left(2/3\right)} = 0.58238\ldots$

- **Fractions and Numbers with Negative Fractional Exponents, page 41**

- $5^{\left(\frac{-3}{4}\right)} = 0.299069\ldots$

- $\left(\frac{6}{7}\right)^{-\left(\frac{4}{5}\right)} = 1.1312469\ldots$

- $\left(-3\left(\frac{4}{5}\right)\right)^{-\left(\frac{4}{3}\right)} = 0.31120866\ldots$

- $\left(3\frac{-7}{11}\right)^{\frac{-4}{5}} = 0.50249931000\ldots$

- $-2\left(7\frac{4}{5}\right)^{\frac{-2}{3}} = -0.50851089\ldots$

- $\left(-2\left(\frac{-9}{16}\right)\right)^{\frac{-4}{7}} = 0.934910\ldots$

- $\left(\frac{4}{9}\right)^{\left(-9/4\right)} = 6.200270\ldots$

- **Word Problems and Mixed Fraction Problems, page 42**
- Flag pole is increased by 4 feet to a total of **16 feet**
- Fish pond contains **1,122.075 gallons** when filled **3/4 full**
- Fish pond contains **1,309.0875 gallons** when filled **7/8 full**

- $5/8 \div 3/4 = \dfrac{5}{6}$

- **26 girls altogether in the 5th and 6th grade classes combined**
- **16 boys in 6th grade classes**

- $\sqrt[4]{\left(2\right)^5} = 2.37841\ldots$

- $\left[\sqrt[4]{2}\right]^5 = \left(1.189207\ldots\right)^5 = 2.37841\ldots$

- **Fraction is 2500 / 3125 = 4/5 of total miles**

CPSIA information can be obtained
at www.ICGtesting.com
Printed in the USA
BVHW091543210921
617191BV00010B/656